Ordnance Survey

THE COTSWOLDS

Pathfinder®Guides

Short Walks

Revised by

~~Jon Kelsall~~

GW00500523

Text: Originally compiled by John Brooks. Revised text for 2006 edition, Tom Hutton; for 2009 to 2017 editions, Nick Channer; for 2020 edition, Dennis and Jan Kelsall

Photography: John Brooks, Nick Channer. Cover: © Paul Felix Photography/Alamy Stock Photo

Design: Ark Creative (UK) Ltd

This product includes mapping data licensed from Ordnance Survey © Crown copyright and database rights (2020) OS 150002047

ISBN: 978-0-31909-080-0

While every care has been taken to ensure the accuracy of the route directions, the publishers cannot accept responsibility for errors or omissions, or for changes in details given. The countryside is not static: hedges and fences can be removed, stiles can be replaced by gates, field boundaries can alter, footpaths can be rerouted and changes in ownership can result in the closure or diversion of some concessionary paths. Also, paths that are easy and pleasant for walking in fine conditions may become slippery, muddy and difficult in wet weather, while stepping stones across rivers and streams may become impassable.

If you find an inaccuracy in either the text or maps, please write to Crimson Publishing at the address below.

First published 2001 by Jarrold Publishing.
Revised and reprinted 2006.

This edition first published in Great Britain 2009 by Crimson Publishing and reprinted with amendments in 2014, 2017 and 2020.

Crimson Publishing, 19-21D Charles Street, Bath, BA1 1HX

www.pathfinderwalks.co.uk

Printed in India by Replika Press Pvt. Ltd. 7/20

Front cover: The Devil's Chimney, Leckhampton Hill
Previous page: Blockley

Contents

Keymap

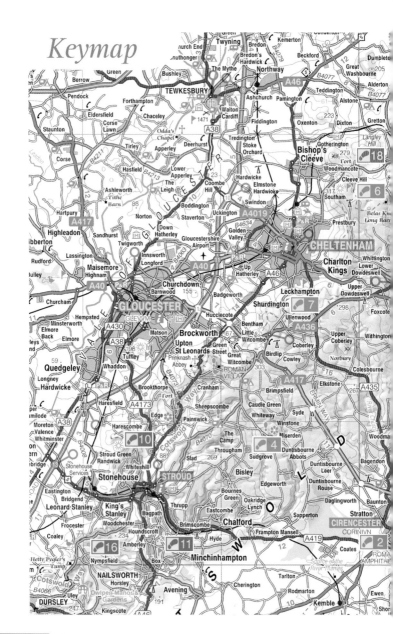

SCALE 1:263 157 or 1 INCH to about 4¼ MILES *1CM to 2.6KM*

```
0       2       4       6       8      10  KILOMETRES     15
```

```
0              2              4        6   MILES    8            10
```

KEYMAP HEIGHTS SHOWN IN METRES

At-a-glance

1	2	3	4

Sherborne Park	*Cirencester Town and Park*	*Eastleach Turville & Eastleach Martin*	*Misarden Park*
• **Magnificent trees** • **pleasure grounds** • **ice-house** • **estate village**	• **Roman Museum** • **church** • **15th-C houses** • **yew hedge**	• **Stone footbridge** • **river wildlife** • **two churches** • **water meadows**	• **Beautiful park** • **splendid trees** • **waterfowl** • **woodland trail**
Walk Distance 2½ miles (4km)	**Walk Distance** 2½ miles (4km)	**Walk Distance** 2½ miles (4km)	**Walk Distance** 3 miles (4.8km). Shorter version 1¾ miles (2.8km)
Time 2 hours	**Time** 1½ hours	**Time** 2 hours	**Time** 2 hours (1 hour for shorter version)
Refreshments None	**Refreshments** Pubs and tearooms in Cirencester	**Refreshments** The Victoria Inn at Eastleach Turville	**Refreshments** The Carpenters Arms at Miserden
A parkland and woodland walk; easy going	A level walk through the market town, dating from Roman times; and a beautiful park (open 08.00–17.00)	Village, lane and riverside walking; mud possible at point **C**; dogs should be kept on the lead	Some short, steep stretches, which may be slippery and muddy; the shorter walk is mostly on secure surfaces
p. 16	**p. 20**	**p. 24**	**p. 28**
Walk Completed ☐	Walk Completed ☐	Walk Completed ☐	Walk Completed ☐

5	**6**	**7**	**8**

Chedworth	*Cleeve Hill*	*Leckhampton Hill*	*Sezincote from Bourton-on-the-Hill*

• Pretty village	• Iron Age fort	• Devil's Chimney	• Pretty village
• secluded meadow	• great views	• extensive views	• lake views
• Roman Villa	• good picnic spot	• Iron Age fort	• country house
• beautiful woodland	• highest point	• Cotswold Way	• meadows

Walk Distance	**Walk Distance**	**Walk Distance**	**Walk Distance**
$2\frac{1}{2}$ miles (4km)	$3\frac{1}{4}$ miles (5.2km)	$3\frac{1}{2}$ miles (5.6km)	$3\frac{1}{2}$ miles (5.6km)
Time	**Time**	**Time**	**Time**
2 hours	2 hours	2 hours	2 hours
Refreshments	**Refreshments**	**Refreshments**	**Refreshments**
Seven Tuns inn at Chedworth	Golf club welcomes visitors for lunches and light refreshments	None en route	Horse and Groom at Bourton-on-the-Hill

Paths are steep in places and will be muddy in winter	Good walking mainly on springy turf with very little climbing; starting close to the top of the hill and following contours. *Do not attempt the route in mist and watch out for golfers*	The gradients are not severe *but there is a rocky staircase that may be slippery*	Grassy walking without severe gradients; some mud in wet weather

p.32	**p. 36**	**p. 40**	**p. 44**
Walk Completed ☐	Walk Completed ☐	Walk Completed ☐	Walk Completed ☐

9

10

11

12

Chastleton from Adlestrop

Haresfield Beacon

Minchinhamp -ton Common

Snowshill

• Lovely village • superb views • historic house • dovecote	• Iron Age fort • quiet lanes • woodland • viewpoints	• Attractive village • outstanding views • open common • earthworks	• Hillside village • famous manor • beauty spot • splendid views

Walk Distance
3½ miles (5.6km)

Time
2 hours

Refreshments
None en route

Walk Distance
3½ miles (5.6km)

Time
2½ hours

Refreshments
None en route

Walk Distance
4 miles (6.4km)

Time
2½ hours

Refreshments
Pubs in Minchinhampton

Walk Distance
4 miles (6.4km)

Time
2½ hours

Refreshments
Snowshill Arms in Snowshill

No taxing gradients. Because some of the tracks are used by horses, parts will be muddy after wet weather

Some climbing to viewpoints; ridge walk; steep descent

Good going on footpaths; quiet lanes and grass

Paths may be muddy after wet weather or if they have been overused by riders. Although there are short sections uphill, none of the gradients is unduly taxing

p. 48 | p. 53 | p. 57 | p. 61

Walk Completed ☐

Walk Completed ☐

Walk Completed ☐

Walk Completed ☐

13

Batsford from Blockley

14

Lost village of Widford from Burford

15

Farmington from Northleach

16

Woodchester Park

• Lovely views • wonderful trees • pretty village • interesting church	• Lost village • isolated church • fine manor house • beautiful river	• Beautiful church • quiet lake • cross-country trail • rolling farmland	• Five lakes • boathouse • Mansion • woodland paths

Walk Distance
4½ miles (7.2km)

Time
2½ hours

Refreshments
Village Shop and Café, and two pubs at Blockley, tearoom at Batsford

Walk Distance
4½ miles (7.2km)

Time
2 hours

Refreshments
Pub and cafés at Burford, pub at Fulbrook

Walk Distance
5 miles (8km)
Shorter version
4 miles (7.2km)

Time
3 hours (2 hours for shorter route)

Refreshments
Pub and cafés in Northleach

Walk Distance
5 miles (8km)

Time
3 hours

Refreshments
None en route; Rose and Crown in Nympsfield

Short, steep sections; going may be muddy in places

Riverside walking with a few gradients and a succession of stiles; riverside may be wet

May be short sections across cultivated land; lack of waymarks

Paths through the National Trust estate are well maintained; a few gradients may be taxing; picnic tables

p.65

Walk Completed ☐

p. 70

Walk Completed ☐

p. 75

Walk Completed ☐

p. 80

Walk Completed ☐

17

The Slaughters from Bourton-on-the-Water

- Mill and museum
- riverside walking
- long-distance trails
- famous villages

Walk Distance
5 miles (8km)
Time
2½ hours
Refreshments
Old Mill tearoom at Lower Slaughter; pubs and cafés in Bourton-on-the-Water

Stretches may be muddy; steady climb out of valley

18

Winchcombe and Hailes Abbey

- Historic town
- Puck Pit lane
- medieval abbey
- delightful country

Walk Distance
5 miles (8km)
Time
3 hours
Refreshments
Pubs and tearooms in Winchcombe

Comparatively easy going outward but the return is more demanding with steady climbs and muddy descents

19

Guiting Wood

- Picturesque valley
- woodland walk
- medieval village
- verdant country

Walk Distance
6¼ miles (10.1km)
Time
3½ hours
Refreshments
The Farmers Arms and The Hollow Bottom at Guiting Power

Some steeper and potential muddy paths in the woodland section

20

Bibury and Coln St Aldwyns

- Pretty village
- lovely riverside
- medieval cottages
- meadows

Walk Distance
6¾ miles (10.9km)
Time
3½ hours
Refreshments
Pubs at Bibury and Coln St Aldwyns

Some gradients and footpaths across cultivated land

Walk Completed ☐   Walk Completed ☐   Walk Completed ☐   Walk Completed ☐

Introduction

The routes and information in this book have been devised specifically with families and children in mind. All the walks include points of interest as well as a question to provide an objective.

If you, or your children, have not walked before, choose from the shorter walks for your first outings. The purpose is not simply to get from A to B but to enjoy an exploration, which may be just a stroll in the countryside.

The walks are graded by length and difficulty, but few landscapes are truly flat, so even shorter walks may involve some ascent. Details are given under Route Features in the first information box for each route. But the precise nature of the ground underfoot will depend on recent weather conditions. If you do set out on a walk and discover the going is harder than you expected, or the weather has deteriorated, do not be afraid to turn back. The route will always be there another day, when you are fitter or the children are more experienced or the weather is better.

Bear in mind that the countryside also changes. Landmarks may disappear, stiles may become gates, rights of way may be altered. However, with the aid of this book and its maps you should be able enjoy many interesting family walks in the countryside.

Effigy of Sir Lawrence Tanfield, Lord Chief Baron of the Exchequer under James I, in Burford church

The Cotswolds

The name 'Cotswold' has a cosy ring to it, evoking images of cottages, green fields and rolling hills. It derives from Saxon words that, together, give the meaning of wooded hollows hidden amid gentle hills, as true a description of the district today as when it was first coined, some 1,200 years ago.

The landscape and its buildings owe everything to the underlying bedrock, the honey-coloured oolitic limestone that is the hallmark of the Cotswolds and was used not only for unpretentious churches and cottages, but also for Oxford colleges and the elegant façades of Georgian Bath and Regency Cheltenham.

The area covers a considerable area of midland and southern England extending from near Stratford-upon-Avon in the north to Wotton-under-Edge, on the doorstep of Bath, to the south. A steep escarpment runs south-west along this line, giving wonderful views over the plain of the River Severn to the uplands of east Wales, while to the east the land dips more gradually to the Thames Valley.

Early history and the landscape

Prehistoric settlers were probably attracted to the Cotswolds by the ease with which they could walk over the rolling limestone hills. The main evidence of their occupation is seen in the long barrows where they buried their dead, the most famous being those of Belas Knap near Winchcombe and Hetty Pegler's Tump at Uley.

During the Bronze Age, new settlers began building hillforts, another feature of the upland landscape in the Cotswolds. Their presence speaks of further invasions, when villages would take all their livestock and possessions behind the defences – earthen ramparts encircling a timber stockade – in the hope that they would be able to resist a siege.

The Romans found these defences easy to overcome and subsequently set up military headquarters in Gloucester and Cirencester. The villas at Chedworth and Witcombe are both large and luxurious and their owners must have had all of the amenities enjoyed at home.

Bourton-on-the-Hill

The Medieval Cotswolds

Among the animals the Romans introduced were sheep with exceptionally long fleeces, and cloth from these was exported throughout the empire. Many centuries after Roman occupation, these animals – known as Cotswold Lions – brought a new prosperity to the region. At the end of the 12th century wool was being exported to weavers in Flanders and arable land, cultivated by ridge and furrow methods, was left unploughed to create sheep walks. This, with the Black Death, brought about rural depopulation, and many villages were abandoned.

It was soon discovered that Cotswold weavers could also produce cloth of high quality. By the end of the 14th century hardly any wool was exported. Instead, vast quantities of cloth were sent to the quays at Bristol and the wool merchants of the wolds and the weavers who made the cloth in the towns were among the wealthiest men in the kingdom.

The Cotswolds enjoyed many natural advantages in cloth-making. The streams flowing through its valleys were reliable and the climate damp, the latter vital if the wool was to have fine texture. Teasels to raise the nap of the cloth and woad to dye it grew in abundance in the clay soil of the Severn vale and there were also deposits of fuller's earth (important for cleaning and shrinking the finished product) near three of the principal cloth-producing towns – Minchinhampton, Stroud and Dursley.

The medieval wool magnates were not slow in spending the rewards they won from their trade. Most obviously, they gave their thanks to God and sought paths to redemption by endowing abbeys and building or enlarging churches.

The merchants also built fine houses for themselves while the crafts-people they employed were content with more humble homes in the towns and villages where they worked. Many of their cottages, some dating from the 15th and 16th centuries, survive and give the Cotswolds their unique character.

From Tudor to modern times
Cloth-making continued to be an important part of the region's economy until the end of the 19th century with the industry mainly centred on Stroud and neighbouring towns. The greatest change to the landscape and economy in early Tudor times was caused by the abolition of the monasteries. Some adapted monastic buildings into mansions for themselves, others built grand houses for themselves away from the religious foundations. The king had unwittingly introduced a new class into society – the landed gentry – who would

play an increasingly important role in the development of the Cotswold countryside.

The infamous Inclosure Acts gave landlords the right to enclose common land. Previously the commons had been where village dwellers had the right to graze their livestock, gather firewood and cultivate small plots. When these privileges were withdrawn, cottagers were often unable to pay rent and were evicted. From about 1670 until the mid-19th century there was a steady exodus from the countryside. This continued as machinery was introduced to agriculture, and the process continues today as ever-larger tractors reduce the need for farmhands.

The Cotswolds has an array of stately homes from all periods. Most of them are surrounded by areas of parkland laid out when the houses were built, and walking through them is a delight.
All that remains is to wish the reader happy walking. May the weather be fair and the going good – whatever the season there is always fresh beauty to be found in the countryside of the Cotswolds, and there is no better way of seeing it than on foot.

This book includes a list of waypoints alongside the description of the walk, so that you can enjoy the full benefits of gps should you wish to.
  For more information about route navigation, improving your map reading ability, walking with a GPS and for an introduction to basic map and compass techniques, read Pathfinder® Guide *Navigation Skills for Walkers* by outdoor writer Terry Marsh (ISBN 978-0-319-09175-3). This title is available in bookshops and online at os.uk/shop

Sherborne Park

- **Magnificent trees**
- **pleasure grounds**
- **ice-house**
- **estate village**

walk 1

The National Trust has done excellent work in opening parts of the Sherborne Park estate to the public. The well-maintained paths lead to many interesting features and each season brings fresh beauty to view. The 4,140-acre (1,675 ha) estate came to the National Trust when Lord Sherborne died in 1982. Sherborne House and stables are not open to the public.

Sherborne House

walk **1**

START National Trust's Ewepen car park, Sherborne	
DISTANCE 2½ miles (4km)	
TIME 2 hours	
PARKING At start – small charge to non-members of National Trust	
ROUTE FEATURES A parkland and woodland walk; easy going	

GPS WAYPOINTS
- 🖊 SP 159 143
- Ⓐ SP 162 141
- Ⓑ SP 166 140
- Ⓒ SP 172 145
- Ⓓ SP 166 148
- Ⓔ SP 164 149

PUBLIC TRANSPORT None	
REFRESHMENTS None	
PUBLIC TOILETS None	
PLAY AREA None	
ORDNANCE SURVEY MAPS Explorer OL45 (The Cotswolds)	

Ewepen Barn, the starting point, was built around 1860, and the surrounding yard was used to shelter sheep in winter, as the name suggests. Almost certainly the barn was also used for winnowing grain after harvest as the main door faces the prevailing wind from the south-west. The barn now serves the National Trust as an information centre.

👟 Turn right out of the car park and on reaching some gates bear slightly right to keep the stone wall on the left. Pass the sports field to come to a point where the drive from the Cheltenham Lodges crosses the track Ⓐ. A beech avenue, magnificent in autumn, leads up to the lodge gates on the A40.

Continue ahead on the track – this point is almost 600ft (183m) above sea level and gives wonderful views northwards. Where a notice tells you that the driveway beyond is private

✳ The **Sherborne estate** originally belonged to Winchcombe Abbey and was bought by Thomas Dutton in 1551 when the abbey was 'dissolved'. Traces of Dutton's house survive in the present building which largely dates from 1829 to 1834 when it was rebuilt for the second Lord Sherborne. The mansion and stables are private, now converted into luxury apartments. The church was rebuilt at the same time as the house, possibly to designs by Anthony Salvin.

The ice-house

B, turn left through an iron gate and keep right at the immediate fork.

The path follows the right-hand edge of Quarry Wood. The quarry, now screened by trees, supplied stone for St Paul's Cathedral and many of the Oxford colleges. Note that a few elms are becoming re-established here among the yews, beeches and oaks.

? Where did the ice for an ice-house come from?

The path leaves the wood to pass the ice-house, which probably dates from the early 19th century.

Larger than it looks from the outside, it was built in a shady place and extends underground.

Bear left by some large stones to a beautiful grassy area surrounding a circular seat made around a yew tree. This is the Pleasure Ground made as a shrubbery where paths wind over miniature hills planted with snowdrops and other bulbs. Return to the main path and veer right at the fork to follow the edge of parkland.

Continue on the path through Sherborne Park to follow railings past a magnificent yew. It was probably growing here when the Duttons came to Sherborne in 1551. Daffodils bloom here, preceded by a display of aconites, and there is a good view of the house and gardens.

The path emerges from the park into the village by the war memorial 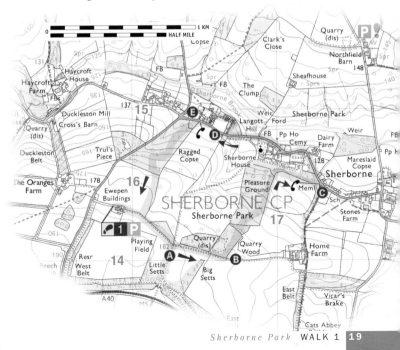. Turn left – there is a view of the lovely Sherborne Brook to the right, which has been widened into lakes flowing over cascades. To the left is the stable block, itself a minor stately home. A path to the church leads up from the end of the stables.

To see the oldest cottages in Sherborne take the path on the right through a green gate D. These are at the western end of the village. The eastern end, beyond the war memorial, was rebuilt as a model village in the mid-19th century.

A lane leads back to the main street. Turn right for a few yards before going left through a gap in the wall E. Farther on, begin climbing and keep right at a bench to the top corner of the wood. The path follows iron railings back to Ewepen Barn. ■

Cirencester Town and Park

■ Roman Museum
■ magnificent church
■ 15th-century houses
■ spectacular yew hedge

Not only is Cirencester the most historic of Cotswold market towns, it can also claim to be the most beautiful with an outstanding church and town houses dating from the 15th century onwards. There is also the extensive park on the west side of the town where people can enjoy the classic view of church and town from Broad Ride.

walk 2

Gazebo in Cirencester Park

START Cirencester church

DISTANCE 2½ miles (4km)

TIME 1½ hours

PARKING Waterloo long-stay car park (walk to church from north end of car park by flats, following river at first, then crossing it and turning left through Abbey Gardens)

ROUTE FEATURES A level walk through the market town, dating from Roman times; and a beautiful park (open 08.00–17.00)

GPS WAYPOINTS

📷 SP 023 020
🅐 SP 021 024
🅑 SP 013 023
🅒 SP 007 023
🅓 SP 019 021

PUBLIC TRANSPORT Tel. 0871 200 2233

REFRESHMENTS Pubs and tearooms in Cirencester

PUBLIC TOILETS At Forum, Corinium and Brewery Arts (Tesco) car parks

PLAY AREA None

ORDNANCE SURVEY MAPS Explorer OL45 (The Cotswolds)

📷 From the church tower, turn right along Gosditch Street into Dollar Street. Note No. 2, bearing the first of several blue civic plaques you will see. This one informs that the abbey mill once stood here. A little farther on Dollar Street House was built for a lawyer, Joseph Pitt, who sponsored Pittsville Spa in Cheltenham early in the 19th century.

Keep ahead into Gloucester Street to pass the White Lion inn.

> **?** *Where did the money to build the tower of St John the Baptist Church come from?*

The vanilla-coloured house on the left dates from the 15th century.

Turn left into Barton Lane before the Nelson inn 🅐. The battlements seen beyond the playing fields on the left belong to the Old Barracks on Cecily Hill, built in 1857. Continue down the lane to cross a bridge and enter Cirencester Park. Note that the park is closed to visitors at 17.00.

Turn left at a T-junction in front of a grand barn, and follow this surfaced track along to a junction of tracks in a clearing. Turn sharp right, and follow this tarmac track down, with some buildings on the left. Shortly after the last of these, you'll climb a short hill to an abandoned farm building. Turn left opposite it **B** and then fork right when the track divides on to North Terrace, which heads westwards with woodland to the left, and to open countryside on the right.

> Three Roman roads meet at Cirencester – Ermine Street, the Fosse Way and Akeman Street – and their town, Corinium Dubunnorum, grew out of an army outpost to become prosperous, second only to London in size and influence. The **Corinium Museum** is the place to learn about Roman life here in the 2nd century AD, with a reconstruction of a mosaics workshop and a host of artefacts on display.

After ½ mile (800m) follow the track to the left **C** past two 'No dogs' notices (which do not seem to apply to these few yards of muddy track) and turn left down Broad Ride.

Broad Ride, Cirencester Park

The vista of church and town at the end of the drive becomes ever more impressive as you approach the park gates. These give on to Cecily Hill with its romantic array of houses, all different but all built of Cotswold stone.

Turn right into Park Street **D** and at the next junction turn left to pass the Corinium Museum – but pause to look back at the 40ft- (12m) high yew hedge planted in 1720 which, with

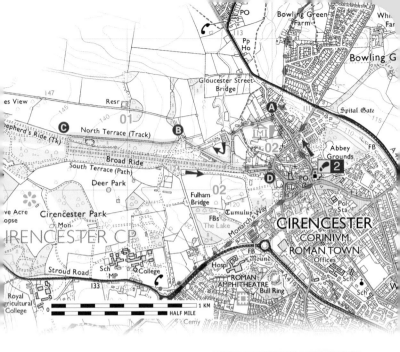

a stone wall, separates Lord Bathurst's mansion from the town. It is one of the highest yew hedges in the world.

Fork left down Black Jack Street to pass a succession of inviting shops and reach the church. Climb the church tower for a view of Cirencester Park. The house was built between 1714 and 1718 for Lord Bathurst, friend and sponsor of the poet Alexander Pope. The tower also gives a spectacular view of the streets and parkland covered in the walk.

St John the Baptist Church is one of the largest parish churches in England and the earliest work dates from the mid-13th century (though a Norman church was here previously and replaced a large Saxon church). Its numerous chapels were built by wool merchants seeking redemption for earthly sins. The enormous south porch – once used as a town hall and as high as the roof of the church – was added in 1490. There is also outstanding medieval glass and the famous Boleyn Cup, made for Anne Boleyn's family and given to the church in 1561.

Eastleach Turville and Eastleach Martin

- Stone footbridge
- river wildlife
- village with two churches
- waterside meadows

walk 3

> Until 1935 Eastleach was officially two separate villages with the River Leach running between them. The river gives the place its character, as do the churches standing on each bank. Upstream from Eastleach it is particularly beautiful (though apt to overflow in winter).

The River Leach at Eastleach

walk 3

START Eastleach Turville (village noticeboard opposite almshouses)

DISTANCE 2½ miles (4km)

TIME 2 hours

PARKING On-road parking in village. Patrons of The Victoria inn are welcome to use pub car park

ROUTE FEATURES Village, lane and riverside walking; mud possible at point **C**; dogs should be kept on the lead

GPS WAYPOINTS
📍 SP 200 051
Ⓐ SP 202 052
Ⓑ SP 208 056
Ⓒ SP 199 064

PUBLIC TRANSPORT None

REFRESHMENTS The Victoria Inn at Eastleach Turville

PUBLIC TOILETS None

PLAY AREA None

ORDNANCE SURVEY MAPS Explorer OL45 (The Cotswolds)

📍 From the centre of Eastleach Turville walk down the road and cross the river by the stone footbridge. Daffodils line the bank and provide a foreground for pictures of St Andrew's Church. The footpath goes through the other churchyard, where the 12th-century Church of St Michael and St Martin is in the care of the Churches Conservation Trust. Its interior preserves relics of an earlier age, like oil lamps and ancient benches.

> ❓ Where is the clock tower in Eastleach?

Turn left out of the church gate and then right on to the lane to Holwell **Ⓐ**. Follow this for nearly a mile (1.6km) with the River Leach to the left.

Turn off the lane to the left just as it begins to climb **Ⓑ**, going through a gate bearing a Hatherop estate notice (dogs to be on leads). The lovely riverside footpath follows the side of the valley where you may well find a heron fishing, or even a kingfisher.

Pass stepping stones that take a path across the river and could be part of a short cut (though, if the river is high, access to them will be difficult and they may even be submerged). Go through a gate and keep

Stone footbridge spanning the River Leach

ahead with a wall and a wood to the right and the river close to the left.

Cross a stile, go through a gate to the next stile and then turn left to follow the field path as it crosses the river by a footbridge **C**. The approaches to the bridge may be muddy. Cross the bridge and turn left by a wall to head south.

The Keble family settled in Eastleach Turville in Tudor times and its most famous member, **John Keble** (1792–1866), served both churches as curate when he was a young priest. Later he became Professor of Poetry at Oxford and was a founder of the Oxford Movement, which believed that the Church of England should be an evangelical institution rather than a political one. Keble College at Oxford was founded by his supporters as a memorial.

This is lovely walking with views of the river below. After ½ mile (800m) there is the first in a succession of steel gates and the river is hidden. Continue to walk with the wall close to the right.

When the buildings of Eastleach Turville can be seen ahead, beyond a final meadow, keep ahead to a steel gate by a children's playground.

Turn right at a lane and then immediately left down a footpath heading for the tower that embellishes a group of estate cottages. The footpath reaches the car park of The Victoria inn. Descend to the road below the pub and turn left back to the village centre and the starting point. ■

The River Leach in flood

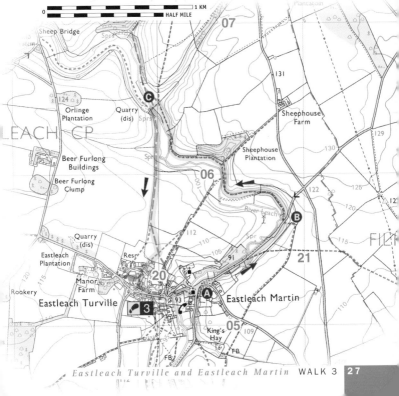

Misarden Park

- Beautiful parkland
- splendid trees
- waterfowl
- woodland trail

walk 4

The parkland trees and wonderful lake are highlights of both routes (the shorter one follows a woodland trail made by the estate and a leaflet giving information about trees and wildlife is available from the gardens and estate office). The longer route is on rights of way that follow woodland paths and tracks as well as a stretch of quiet lane.

Misarden Park Lake

walk 4

START Miserden village centre

DISTANCE 3 miles (4.8km). Shorter version 1¾ miles (2.8km)

TIME 2 hours (1 hour for shorter route)

PARKING On-street parking in village

ROUTE FEATURES Some short, steep stretches, which may be slippery and muddy; the shorter walk is mostly on secure surfaces

GPS WAYPOINTS
SO 937 088
Ⓐ SO 939 090
Ⓑ SO 943 093
Ⓒ SO 946 094
Ⓓ SO 954 093
Ⓔ SO 944 087

PUBLIC TRANSPORT Tel. 0871 200 2233

REFRESHMENTS The Carpenters Arms at Miserden

PUBLIC TOILETS None

PLAY AREA None

ORDNANCE SURVEY MAPS Explorer 179 (Gloucester, Cheltenham & Stroud), Landranger 163 (Cheltenham & Cirencester)

From the centre of the village (where a large tree supports an octagonal shelter) turn your back to the Carpenters' Arms and walk downhill past the estate office and nursery and through a gate into the park. Stick with the drive for 125 yds and then bear off right Ⓐ. If you reach a sharp bend, you have gone too far. Slant across the sloping parkland to a stone stile into a wood. A path leads on through the trees, soon reaching an intersection of drives. Cross a stream to join the drive ahead; this follows the stream to a bridge spanning the River Frome Ⓑ.

At this point, those undertaking the shorter walk can, after crossing the bridge, turn off right at a green waymark to follow the little river below the slopes of a Norman motte-and-bailey castle. The path goes beneath some magnificent Douglas firs that were planted in Victorian times, and then crosses a small stream before coming to a woodland track.

Bear right on to this (it may be muddy after wet weather) and follow it along the edge of the wood to Misarden Park Lake, a beautiful

> **?** Can you detect what animal has been climbing over the stone stile leading into the wood in the first paragraph?

stretch of water in a perfect setting that was created in the 18th century. Kingfishers are regular visitors as well as heron and several varieties of waterfowl.

Cross the bridge over the outfall with care and turn right on to the drive to walk on the other side of the lake. Go left at a T-junction and climb

The lake in winter

towards the house. An unusual avenue of western red cedars leads up to the house while elsewhere many rare trees have been planted. Towards the top, just before passing through a low wall, turn off right by a waymark to a fence stile into a meadow. Follow the top wall to the corner to find a low wall stile discretely set just to the right (not the one in the corner). Over that, bear left and head away across the park to regain the main drive. Follow it left to return to the park entrance and the village centre.

To continue on the main route, climb up the hill beyond the bridge for ¼ mile (400m). Where the drive swings sharply right **C**, look for faint yellow marks on the trees indicating a path off left. Cross a small causeway and climb up 50 yds to another path off right, again indistinctly marked with a stencilled yellow arrow. Higher up, ignore an overgrown crossing track and wind on up to a stone stile at the top of the wood. Turn left at the edge of a field to reach a quiet lane. Follow it to the right for about ½ mile (800m) to a gate lodge **D**. A bridleway sign points the way along the grand driveway.

However, where it subsequently swings right towards gateposts topped by stone eagles, keep ahead on a track. Ignore the two tracks immediately leaving left and continue forward in a steep decent, which can be slippery. Towards the bottom as you pass a magnificent beech, the sound of a waterfall heralds your approach to a lake. Cross the outfall from the lake and turn left onto a drive.

Climb away for about 75 yds. As the drive levels **E**, turn right at a footpath sign to follow a grassy track rising to a field gate and stile. Beyond this go a few steps to the right for a glimpse back to the lake surrounded by wooded hills. Continue upwards along a sunken track through pasture to another gate and stile, which opens onto a lane. Head right for 300 yds, but where the lane then swings left take the footpath on the right between a fence and stone wall. Carry on over a stile, shortly emerging past cottages back at the village centre by the former school. ■

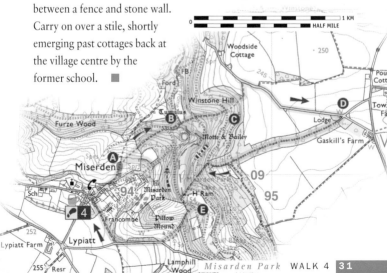

Chedworth

■ Picturesque village   ■ Roman Villa
■ secluded meadow   ■ beautiful woodland

Chedworth is one of the more remote Cotswold villages. Its cottages are strung along a deep, wooded valley. The famous Roman Villa was built in the neighbouring valley, and visitors can see its mosaics, two bathhouses and fascinating artefacts displayed in a museum.

walk 5

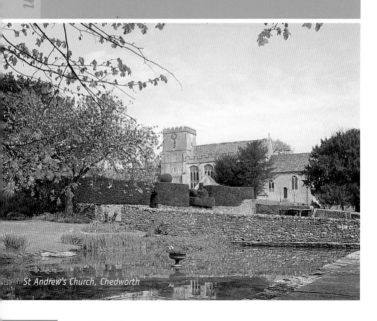
St Andrew's Church, Chedworth

walk 5

START Seven Tuns inn, Chedworth

DISTANCE 2½ miles (4km)

TIME 2 hours

PARKING Seven Tuns car park – alternatively you may prefer to start from the Roman Villa and use the woodland walks car park there (closed in winter)

ROUTE FEATURES Paths are steep in places and will be muddy in winter

GPS WAYPOINTS
   SP 052 119
Ⓐ SP 053 122
Ⓑ SP 050 132
Ⓒ SP 055 134
Ⓓ SP 055 124

PUBLIC TRANSPORT
Tel. 0871 200 2233

REFRESHMENTS Seven Tuns inn at Chedworth

PUBLIC TOILETS At Roman Villa

PLAY AREA None

ORDNANCE SURVEY MAPS
Explorer OL45 (The Cotswolds)

Take the footpath opposite the Seven Tuns to pass the church. The pub dates from 1610 while the airy church lit by Perpendicular windows has a Norman tower. Keep ahead when the road swings right, following a sign to the Roman Villa.

Cross a stile at the end of the cul-de-sac Ⓐ and bear slightly left. The track of the railway line that once connected Chedworth with Cheltenham and Cirencester lies on the other side of the fence.

> **?** *What type of deity was the shrine in the Roman Villa dedicated to?*

Head up a long meadow to climb to a stile into woodland located about 75 yds from the corner. A flight of steps takes the path to the top of a steep bank. Keep ahead across a bridleway.

The path now follows a field edge and then crosses arable land towards Chedworth Woods. The descent into the woods may be slippery after wet weather, but after this the way is clear on level ground for a short distance before another steep descent to a crossways Ⓑ.

Turn right and continue to descend, going beneath the old railway line. A path on the right leads into the Gloucestershire Wildlife Trust's nature reserve and the one ahead goes to the Roman Villa.

Roman mosaic at the villa

> **Chedworth Roman Villa**
> was one of the largest villas in England, and more than a mile (1.6km) of its walls can still be traced. Visitors to the villa will see fine mosaics, a shrine to a deity, the central heating system, two bath-houses and even the latrine. A museum has a display of objects found on the site, which is in the care of the National Trust; tel. 01242 890256 for times of opening.

The walk continues by walking down the driveway from the villa, lined by impressive yew trees. Turn right **C** on to a bridleway just as the drive bends left by a sign for Chedworth Roman Villa. When the track divides, fork left and begin to climb. After about ½ mile (800m) join a farm track at the top to reach a fiveways **D**.

Keep ahead to follow the Monarch's Way sign to pass a cattle yard and reach a road. Turn right and at the first bend go left on to an enclosed footpath that descends to Chedworth. Drop down the field after a gate and a broken stile.

Cross a road by a row of cottages and go down to a stream crossed by a stone bridge. After a stone stile the path climbs to a wooden one that takes it across the old railway embankment. Bear right after another stile to follow the top of a field and then walk past stables to a road back by the Seven Tuns.

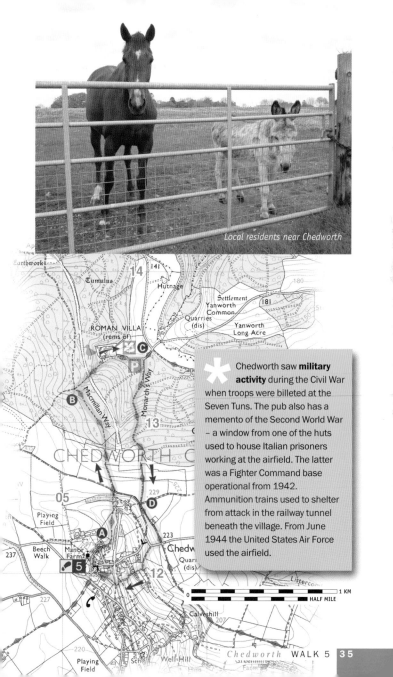

Local residents near Chedworth

Chedworth saw **military activity** during the Civil War when troops were billeted at the Seven Tuns. The pub also has a memento of the Second World War – a window from one of the huts used to house Italian prisoners working at the airfield. The latter was a Fighter Command base operational from 1942. Ammunition trains used to shelter from attack in the railway tunnel beneath the village. From June 1944 the United States Air Force used the airfield.

Cleeve Hill

- Iron Age fort
- great views
- good picnic spot
- Cotswolds' highest point

walk 6

Cheltenham owes its origins to mineral-rich springs with supposed healing properties. In tandem with this natural asset its situation, sheltered by high ground to the north and east, must also have been beneficial to health. The climb to the summit of Cleeve Hill from the town centre would be arduous and time-consuming whereas the walk described here involves little climbing.

Sheep near the houses of Nutterswood

START Cleeve Hill, golf clubhouse

DISTANCE 3¼ miles (5.2km)

TIME 2 hours

PARKING Park in disused quarry just beyond clubhouse; alternative car park at point **Ⓐ**

ROUTE FEATURES Good walking mainly on springy turf with very little climbing; starting close to the top of the hill and following contours. *Do not attempt the route in mist and watch out for golfers*

GPS WAYPOINTS
🔲 SO 989 272
Ⓐ SO 985 268
Ⓑ SO 982 257
Ⓒ SO 986 253
Ⓓ SO 987 256

PUBLIC TRANSPORT
Tel. 0871 200 2233

REFRESHMENTS Golf club welcomes visitors for meals and light refreshments

PUBLIC TOILETS By main road near point **Ⓐ**

PLAY AREA None

ORDNANCE SURVEY MAPS
Explorer 179 (Gloucester, Cheltenham & Stroud), Landranger 163 (Cheltenham & Cirencester)

🔲 Turn left from the quarry car park and walk in front of the clubhouse along the lower edge of Cleeve Common. The track drops down close to the road **Ⓐ**, where there are public toilets.

The summit of **Cleeve Hill** is the highest point in the Cotswolds at 1,083ft (330m) above sea-level. Its position on the edge of the steep escarpment overlooking the Vale of Severn makes it a wonderful view-point and keen eyes will identify Gloucester, Tewkesbury, the Malverns and Bredon Hill.

Continue along the track that runs along the eastern edge of Cleeve Common, to pass above a hotel car park, overlooked by a castellated tower, and come to crossways with a cattle-grid to your right. Bear half-left onto the upper of two lanes. The Ring – an Iron Age fort – can be seen on the left.

Famous sportsmen used to train on Cleeve Common, one of whom is said to haunt Prestbury, just below the hill. Can you work out which sport?

Stay on the track, which becomes asphalted for a short distance, and climb to the corner of Thrift Wood. The fine beech trees here are glorious in the autumn. Follow the track alongside woodland, bending right, then left to several boulders **B** . Take the higher path, and follow it above the huddle of houses at Nutterswood. The going becomes grassy as it passes below rock faces up to the left, topped with another Iron Age fort.

Both upper and lower tracks lead up to the same point on Huddlestone's Table, a level, grassy area which is a great viewpoint as well as being a good picnic place. Stay on the track to climb a short, steep hill, and at the top the path divides **C**.

Veer away from the wall and then turn left onto a path, in line with an information board and waymark to the right. Continue on the path to a junction with a path coming from radio masts.

Turn left here to make for a lone tree protected by a paling **D**. From here the way lies across the golf course, the objective being the summit

A frosty morning on Cleeve Hill

of Cleeve Hill, topped by a triangulation pillar and a view-indicator.

From the summit, drop left, past the view indicator, and locate a clear path that contours along the side of the hill, past a seat. From here the clubhouse can be clearly

The Iron Age earthworks scattered around Cleeve Common are easily explained today, as are the deep troughs lower down, caused by the spring line. However, our ancestors believed that both features were caused by sea erosion at the time when **Noah's Ark** was adrift in the Flood.

seen. The path passes above two former quarries before joining a clear, chalky track that leads back to the clubhouse and car park. ■

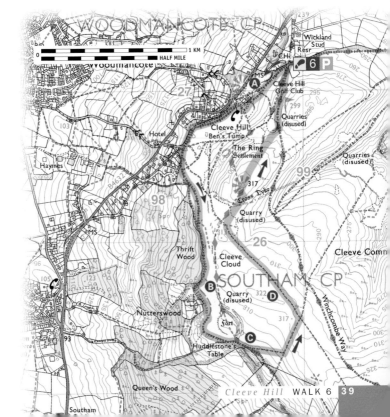

Leckhampton Hill

■ Devil's Chimney ■ Iron Age fort
■ extensive views ■ scenic Cotswold Way

walk 7

Leckhampton is a suburb on the south side of Cheltenham and its hill is where much of the limestone used in building the elegant houses came from. In 1929 the town council bought the 400-acre (162 ha) hilltop to stop further quarrying and since then it has become a favourite venue for locals and visitors. There is no finer viewpoint for the spa and surrounding countryside.

On the Cotswold Way across Hartley Hill

walk 7

START Leckhampton Hill car park

DISTANCE 3½ miles (5.6km)

TIME 2 hours

PARKING At start

ROUTE FEATURES The gradients are not severe *but there is a rocky staircase that may be slippery*

GPS WAYPOINTS
🖍 SO 950 180
Ⓐ SO 947 176
Ⓑ SO 950 185
Ⓒ SO 958 185
Ⓓ SO 965 179
Ⓔ SO 966 177

PUBLIC TRANSPORT None

REFRESHMENTS None en route

PUBLIC TOILETS None

PLAY AREA None

ORDNANCE SURVEY MAPS Explorer 179 (Gloucester, Cheltenham & Stroud), Landranger 163 (Cheltenham & Cirencester)

🖍 Leave the car park and turn right at the lane. When the lane begins to descend steeply leave it to the right on to a footpath with a Cotswold Way sign Ⓐ.

A quarry, used as a car park, lies below the path which climbs gently with a wonderful view before you. The Devil's Chimney is best seen before you reach the top, lower paths giving excellent views of it.

> **?** *Can you guess how many people once huddled on the summit of the Devil's Chimney?*

Beyond the Chimney the topmost path rises to the summit, where there are sparse remains of an Iron Age fort. Keep to the top path which passes a view-indicator and then a triangulation pillar sited on the ramparts of the fort. A maze of paths covers this part of the hill.

Follow the path just to the left of the triangulation pillar, which goes through a spinney of pine trees to reach a surfaced drive Ⓑ. Take the rough path to the left of this along to a gate by some silver birch trees. Do not go through it; instead, keep ahead, following the Cotswold Way with views of Cheltenham on the left. Keep right when the path forks **C**, still on the Cotswold Way, and begin a steady descent down a spur towards the main road, twisting through gorse.

There is a rocky staircase and a cycle barrier before the path reaches open land. Keep ahead along the hedgerow and at the end turn left to a T-junction **D**.

Palaeontologists have been hammering fossils out of the exposed layers of **oolitic limestone** here for many years to the point where considerable damage has been caused. The top layer of limestone is known as ragstone and was used for walls, cottages and farm buildings. The best quality of material, freestone, is of finer grain and lies below the ragstone.

Former quarry near the Devil's Chimney

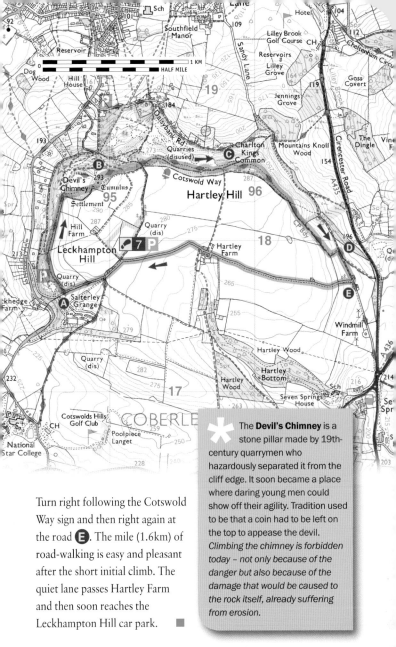

Turn right following the Cotswold Way sign and then right again at the road **E**. The mile (1.6km) of road-walking is easy and pleasant after the short initial climb. The quiet lane passes Hartley Farm and then soon reaches the Leckhampton Hill car park. ∎

The **Devil's Chimney** is a stone pillar made by 19th-century quarrymen who hazardously separated it from the cliff edge. It soon became a place where daring young men could show off their agility. Tradition used to be that a coin had to be left on the top to appease the devil. *Climbing the chimney is forbidden today – not only because of the danger but also because of the damage that would be caused to the rock itself, already suffering from erosion.*

Sezincote from Bourton-on-the-Hill

- Picturesque village
- lake views
- fine country house
- meadows and parkland

walk 8

Bourton-on-the-Hill is a picture book village when viewed from this walk, though it suffers from being bisected by a major road. The walk follows rights of way through meadows and parkland and passes Sezincote, a unique mansion with famous gardens in an idyllic setting.

Bourton-on-the-hill

walk 8

START Bourton-on-the-Hill

DISTANCE 3½ miles (5.6km)

TIME 2 hours

PARKING On-road parking on byway to south of A44

ROUTE FEATURES Grassy walking without severe gradients; some mud in wet weather

GPS WAYPOINTS
- 🖉 SP 175 324
- Ⓐ SP 174 322
- Ⓑ SP 179 321
- Ⓒ SP 182 314
- Ⓓ SP 175 307
- Ⓔ SP 174 313

PUBLIC TRANSPORT Buses from Cirencester, Bourton-on-the-Water, Stow-on-the-Wold, Cheltenham, Chipping Campden and Moreton-in-Marsh.
Tel. 0871 200 2233

REFRESHMENTS Horse and Groom at Bourton-on-the-Hill

PUBLIC TOILETS None

PLAY AREA None

ORDNANCE SURVEY MAPS Explorer OL45 (The Cotswolds)

🖉 From the telephone box at the corner of Bourton-on-the-Hill's back street, walk a few steps westwards and then take the footpath on the left by Smithy Cottage – Bourton's blacksmith must have been prosperous to have such a house. Pass through a gate and descend by a wall to another one Ⓐ.

Go left after this to follow the hedgerow and a small stream through three meadows before turning right at a line of oak trees on to an enclosed footpath Ⓑ which will be muddy after wet weather.

Turn left to walk by the side of a newly planted spinney to a stile that takes the path across a drive and field to a footbridge into a small copse. After this the path continues across farmland following a stream towards a wood. Turn left to cross a footbridge Ⓒ and then walk away from the wood, keeping a hedge and ditch to the right.

Turn right at the end of the meadow on to a surfaced track and come to Upper Rye Farm. Pass to the left of the farm and turn right after a corrugated hay barn to reach the surfaced

? *Can you spot something fearsome observing you on this pleasant walk?*

Farmland near Sezincote House

track coming away from the farm. This is easy walking through splendid countryside. Note the magnificent oak trees.

A short, steady climb takes the route up to the Keepers' Cottages.

Turn right 100 yds after these **D** before the cattle-grid on to a path by the side of a wood. Bear right away from the wood as the lake comes into view on the right. The right of way drops

The dome of **Sezincote** and its orange-coloured stonework show that its builder had Indian connections. Sir Charles Cockerell made his fortune with the East India Company and began the house in 1805. The dome is said to have given the Prince Regent the idea for the Brighton Pavilion. Although the exterior is flamboyant, the interior is restrained and classical. However, the gardens are as spectacular as the outside of the house, and overall it makes Sezincote one of England's most appealing country houses.

down to the meadow between the lake and the house.

After two gates close together the path keeps right to follow a wooden fence. Keep ahead when this ends **E** to follow frequent waymarks through the beautiful park to a pair of wooden kissing-gates. Note the ridge-and-furrow patterns which at one point lie at right angles to one another.

> ✳ St Lawrence's Church has Norman piers even though it looks Perpendicular from the outside. **Bourton-on-the-Hill** has several houses that could almost claim to be mansions, most notably the early 18th-century Bourton House at the bottom end of the village and Manor Farmhouse (of the same period) at the top.

The path is obvious once Bourton-on-the-Hill comes into view, heading directly towards the church. There are grand houses on each flank of the village. The outward route is rejoined at the end of a wall and soon takes you back to the village. ■

Chastleton from Adlestrop

■ Lovely village   ■ historic house
■ superb views   ■ ornamental dovecote

This route is a delightful way of savouring the best Cotswold scenery without taxing gradients. The gently undulating footpaths, bridleways and lanes take you to see a splendid historic house and adjacent church. Keep a look out for foxes and deer.

walk 9

Chastleton House

walk 9

START Adlestrop Village Hall at centre of village nearly opposite a bus shelter featuring the old station nameboard

DISTANCE $3\frac{1}{2}$ miles (5.6km)

TIME 2 hours

PARKING At village hall (contribute to honesty box)

ROUTE FEATURES No taxing gradients. Because some of the tracks are used by horses, parts will be muddy after wet weather

GPS WAYPOINTS
🥾 SP 241 271
Ⓐ SP 245 281
Ⓑ SP 246 287
Ⓒ SP 252 287
Ⓓ SP 253 273
Ⓔ SP 247 271
Ⓕ SP 246 273

PUBLIC TRANSPORT Tel. 0871 200 2233

REFRESHMENTS None en route

PUBLIC TOILETS None

PLAY AREA None

ORDNANCE SURVEY MAPS Explorer OL45 (The Cotswolds)

This field was cultivated in strips in medieval times which has left characteristic **ridges and furrows**. Note how the moles prefer the ridges, probably because of the abundance of worms that are still enjoying the richness in the soil after centuries of organic farming.

Turn left out of the car park and then immediately left again onto a broad track that leads past an equestrian exercise enclosure. Over a stile beside a gate, bear left on a diagonal trod across meadow.

Beyond a stile in the far corner, follow a fence for 50 yds and then climb another stile on the left by a large tree. Follow the hedge right to a stile by the corner Ⓐ. Continue up in the same direction through a large meadow to yet another stile at the top, pausing there to enjoy the distant view towards Stow.

What made the old railway station sign in Adlestrop so well-known?

Pass through a belt of trees and cross a field to the corner of Peasewell Wood Ⓑ. Here a gate opens onto a track through a lime avenue leading to Chastleton, from which there is a view right to a pretty dovecote. Emerging

Chastleton from Adlestrop WALK 9 **49**

onto a lane, follow it right past Chastleton House and the village church.

Leave the lane through a kissing-gate opposite the church and strike past the dovecote to the top corner of the field. Through a gate, follow

Chastleton House was built between 1607 and 1612 by Walter Jones, a wealthy lawyer who acquired the estate from Robert Catesby, one of the conspirators in the Gunpowder Plot. But later generations were never affluent, and the house remained little altered over the centuries. Bought by the National Trust in 1993, they have preserved its unique atmosphere and Jacobean garden, even keeping 40-year-old jars of preserved fruit. (Opening times: www.nationaltrust.org.uk/chastleton-house)

the left hedge down into Peasewell Wood and go left. Emerge at the end onto the bend of a lane **C**. However, ignore it and instead walk right through a kissing-gate, passing out of the trees into the corner of a large meadow. Head away here, beside a rough dividing strip across the flank

Dovecote near Chastleton House

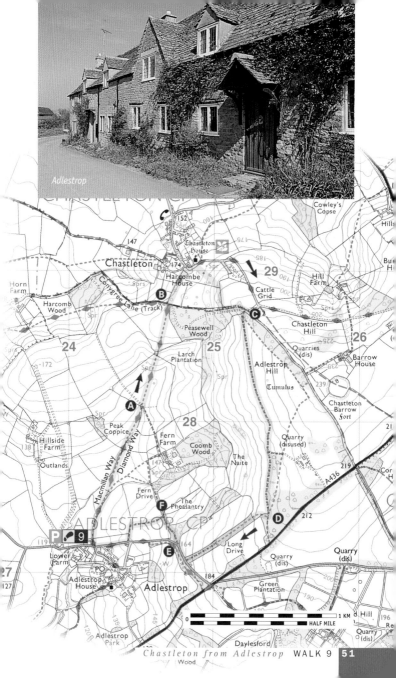

Adlestrop

Adlestrop countryside

of Adlestrop Hill. There are superb views over the outward route to Stow and beyond.

Where the path later divides, bear right, shortly passing beside the lower edge of a wood – you may well see fox or deer here. Remaining in the field, swing with the boundary down to the next corner, where, just to the right, a path leaves into the Long Drive **D**. Head downhill through the trees, coming out at the bottom onto a lane.

Turn right, but where it then bends left, keep ahead **E** on a metalled drive to Fern Farm. After some 250 yds, beneath power cables **F**, leave left to follow a faint margin between two fields. At the bottom, swing left again to join a contained track out to the lane. Follow it right into Adlestrop, finally passing the bus shelter and its famous sign to return to the village hall. Before you leave, you might like to spend a little time exploring this beautiful Cotswold village. ■

Jane Austen (1775-1817) often visited her uncle, who was one time Church rector of Adlestrop, and speculation has it that the house and grounds of Adlestrop Park could have been the setting for her novel *Mansfield Park*.

Haresfield Beacon

- Iron Age fort
- quiet lanes
- glorious woodland
- magnificent viewpoints

Many people park their cars and walk ¼ mile (400m) across springy turf to the view-indicator, admire the view and return to the car park. This route demands more effort, taking you through woodland before climbing to Haresfield Beacon. Then there is a ridge walk and another short climb to get to the view-indicator.

walk 10

Haresfield Beacon

walk 10

START Shortwood car park, on minor road between Painswick and Haresfield

DISTANCE 3½ miles (5.6km)

TIME 2½ hours

PARKING At start

ROUTE FEATURES Some climbing to viewpoints; ridge walk; steep descent

GPS WAYPOINTS

📍 SO 832 086
Ⓐ SO 838 083
Ⓑ SO 841 088
Ⓒ SO 833 094
Ⓓ SO 824 092
Ⓔ SO 824 089
Ⓕ SO 827 087

PUBLIC TRANSPORT Tel. 0871 200 2233

REFRESHMENTS None en route

PUBLIC TOILETS Adjacent to car park

PLAY AREA None

ORDNANCE SURVEY MAPS Explorer 179 (Gloucester, Cheltenham & Stroud), Landranger 163 (Cheltenham & Cirencester)

From the car park turn right onto the road and then turn immediately right again, through a gate, onto a footpath signposted to Randwick, Maiden Hill, Doverow Hill. Walk into the wood, with the road to your left, and a drystone wall to your right. This is the boundary of National Trust land. Keep the wall to the right as the path follows the edge of a field and reaches a road. Climb a stile and turn left, bearing left at a road junction at Bird in Hand and passing Stoneridge Farm before taking the next footpath on the right Ⓐ.

Walk across the large field, heading to the right of the radio masts. Cross the road into woodland and keep ahead to descend steeply – the writer found a stick helpful in managing this safely. Towards the bottom the gradient eases. Turn left Ⓑ on to the track that is part of the Cotswold Way.

Memorial stone near Cliff Well

The going now becomes easy on a pleasant bridleway on the edge of Stockend Wood. When it joins a lane, keep ahead on it as it descends for almost ¼ mile (400m) before turning left **C** on to a bridleway signposted to Haresfield Beacon, where it levels. Note Cliff Well, on the left, with a curiously bent cross on top of the well-house.

A steady climb follows. Where the track bends left there is a

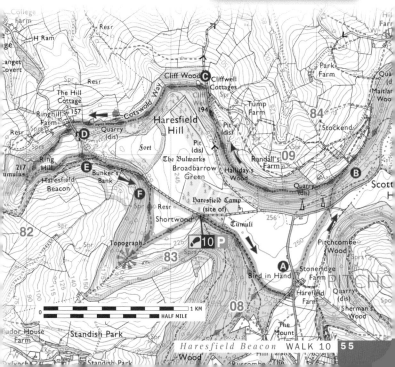

granite memorial stone that commemorates the raising of the Siege of Gloucester by Royalists in 1643 that also testifies to the ancient importance of the track.

After this the walking is easier and the track soon reaches a lane at Ringhill Farm. Turn left and, after 50 yds, right **D** on to a footpath following the Cotswold Way logo past two gates and on to a track climbing up the flank of Ring Hill. Just before the top a stile takes the path on to the triangulation pillar that gives a wonderful view across the Vale of Gloucester and the Forest of Dean to the Brecon Beacons.

> Haresfield Beacon is such a fine vantage point that it was used as a defensive position by prehistoric people and the Romans. Highly defensible, **fortified sites** are common to this wonderfully scenic corner of the Cotswolds and Haresfield Beacon, a popular National Trust beauty spot, is no exception. The site extends to 16 acres and is enclosed by a single rampart and ditch. Explanatory notes and panels give visitors some idea of the importance and significance of Haresfield Beacon in its original role as a fort.

Turn sharp left from the pillar to negotiate the ramparts of the Iron Age fort and follow the ridge eastwards to a stile. A hoard of 3,000 Roman coins was once discovered near the remains of the fort. The path is very well trodden and soon reaches the road **E**. However, turn right a few steps before reaching a National Trust moneybox to descend steps and reach a path that follows a wall. There are fine views to the right and then a steady climb to a footpath junction **F**. Bear right across the grass to head for the view-indicator, which from the distance looks like an upturned drum.

The topograph turns out to be a remarkable work in bronze that shows the rivers and hills of the surrounding area. On a good day you can see the Sugar Loaf Mountain near Abergavenny from here, more than 30 miles (48km) distant. Turn left away from the topograph on the most obvious path to return to the Shortwood car park.

Minchinhampton Common

- Attractive village
- outstanding views
- open common
- prehistoric earthworks

Minchinhampton is a large village on the south-west edge of the Cotswolds where lovely old houses huddle around a picturesque Market House and beautiful church. It occupies a plateau between two deep valleys important for their woollen mills, a trade carried on here from the 17th to late 19th century. The village common is the largest one surviving in the area.

walk 11

Looking towards Besbury Common

START Market House, Minchinhampton

DISTANCE 4 miles (6.4km)

TIME 2½ hours

PARKING Minchinhampton

ROUTE FEATURES Good going on footpaths; quiet lanes and grass

GPS WAYPOINTS

📍 SO 872 007

Ⓐ SO 875 012

Ⓑ SO 869 014

Ⓒ SO 859 014

Ⓓ SO 851 015

Ⓔ SO 860 010

PUBLIC TRANSPORT Tel. 0871 200 2233

REFRESHMENTS Pubs in Minchinhampton

PUBLIC TOILETS Opposite Minchinhampton church in Bell Lane

PLAY AREA None

ORDNANCE SURVEY MAPS Explorer 168 (Stroud, Tetbury & Malmesbury), Landranger 163 (Cheltenham & Cirencester)

👣 From the Market House (1698) walk up Bell Lane past Holy Trinity Church. Turn right to pass the west end of the church and follow the churchyard wall past a parking area and along the eastern side of the common. Where the wall finally finishes, bear right to the corner of the common at the end of Butt Street.

> **?** *To what local trade does Holy Trinity Church owe its size?*

Cross over the main road into The Knapp, but leave after 100 yds for a footpath on the left Ⓐ. Stone stiles take the path across a driveway to an enclosed path past the grounds of a house and surrounding paddocks.

Crossing a stile onto the edge of the escarpment overlooking Besbury Common, turn left and enjoy the wonderful views northwards of winding, wooded valleys and rolling hills from strategically placed seats. Like Minchinhampton Common, this part of Besbury Common is in the care of the National Trust.

Keep ahead as you emerge onto a quiet lane, bearing right at a junction Ⓑ and walking down a hill to pass the Old Weaver's House. The lane ends at a junction by a gate and cattle grid onto the common. Keep ahead for

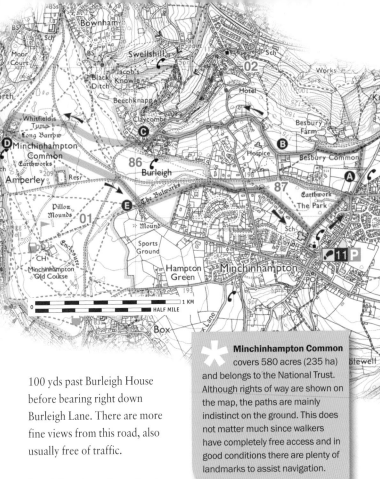

100 yds past Burleigh House before bearing right down Burleigh Lane. There are more fine views from this road, also usually free of traffic.

Bear left at the main road and climb to the common. By the Burleigh village sign **C** turn off right and follow a faint trod behind the houses until you spot a bungalow and a turret with a flag pole on your right. Turn left here, head uphill and approach a mound with trees and bushes. Keep to the right of it, then to the left of a large pit to reach the road.

Cross the next part of the common heading westwards towards a large building half hidden by trees. Pass to the right of the building (a tall

Minchinhampton

semi-detached house) to reach the road, which overlooks the Nailsworth valley.

Go left to a bus shelter **D** ornamented with a weather vane, which stands opposite a small triangular green and the village war memorial. Turn left onto the common and follow a line of low earthworks (part of the extensive Amberley Camp, an Iron Age hillfort) towards a reservoir, a distinctive mound surrounded by a stone wall topped by grey railings. As you approach, however, keep it well to the right so as to reach the middle of an extended junction at Tom Long's Post, where six roads meet.

Walk beside the road ahead, signposted to Minchinhampton town centre. After crossing the line of The Bulwarks **E**, turn off left, heading away parallel to the embankment and deep ditch, making for the distant corner of a wall behind some large houses.

> **Holy Trinity Church** was a Norman church enlarged in the 12th century, but its most glorious feature – the south transept with its enormous window – dates from early in the 14th century. The tower owes its appearance to an unsafe spire that was abbreviated in 1563 when the delightful coronet was added to compensate.

Follow the wall, curving beside The Bulwarks, a rambling Iron Age earthwork enclosing an area of 600 acres (243 ha), which was dug as a defence against the Romans' advance. Cross a road and continue to follow the wall on the perimeter of the common. Holy Trinity Church, with its unique coronet, is soon to be seen ahead and the way back to the village centre is clear. ■

Snowshill

- Hillside village
- famous manor
- beauty spot
- splendid views

Snowshill is famous for its manor, once the home of the eccentric Charles Wade, and as a beauty spot, perched halfway up a hill on the northern edge of the Cotswolds. The delightfully varied route uses footpaths, bridleways and lanes, all of which give splendid views of the village and surrounding countryside.

walk 12

Snowshill from the south

walk 12

START Snowshill

DISTANCE 4 miles (6.4km)

TIME 2½ hours

PARKING Village car park on road to Broadway

ROUTE FEATURES Paths may be muddy after wet weather or if they have been overused by riders. Although there are short sections uphill, none of the gradients is unduly taxing

GPS WAYPOINTS
- 🔎 SP 097 339
- Ⓐ SP 090 336
- Ⓑ SP 083 341
- Ⓒ SP 086 353
- Ⓓ SP 089 352
- Ⓔ SP 087 340

PUBLIC TRANSPORT None

REFRESHMENTS Snowshill Arms in Snowshill

PUBLIC TOILETS None

PLAY AREA None

ORDNANCE SURVEY MAPS Explorer OL45 (The Cotswolds)

👢 Turn right out of the car park and fork right to descend to the village, passing the back of Snowshill Manor, then the pub and the church. Bear right, noting the wall on the right embellished with built-in stone balls and triangles.

A footpath leaves to the right but continue climbing the lane, turning right at the junction near the top. There is a fine view to the right as you pass Sheepscombe. Turn right after this, and after 150 yds go left through an iron gate Ⓐ and climb through the meadow towards the upper part of Littleworth Wood. A stile, hidden at first, goes into the wood at the end of a combe (dry valley).

Go right at the lane, which follows the top of the wood. Bear right about 100yds beyond the end of the wood to follow the Cotswold Way waymarks Ⓑ.

There is an incomparable 180° view as you approach Laverton Hill Barn, where the right of way passes to the left of the modern house.

Broadway is well seen ahead as the track forks. Keep right and begin to descend. Remain on the Cotswold Way when a restricted byway leaves to the left. Broadway Tower can be seen ahead.

Go through a metal gate and follow a fence – Buckland church is seen to the left. Just before a distinctive stone gatepost there is a stile to the left, and a footpath leaves at the gatepost **C** to climb past a waymark post towards the

Snowshill Manor was the home of Charles Wade, a human magpie, who collected curious objects from all over the world. Many of them remain in the beautiful house, which Wade presented to the National Trust in 1951. The manor dates from the early 16th century (with later additions and alterations) while the wonderful terraced garden was laid out in 1919.

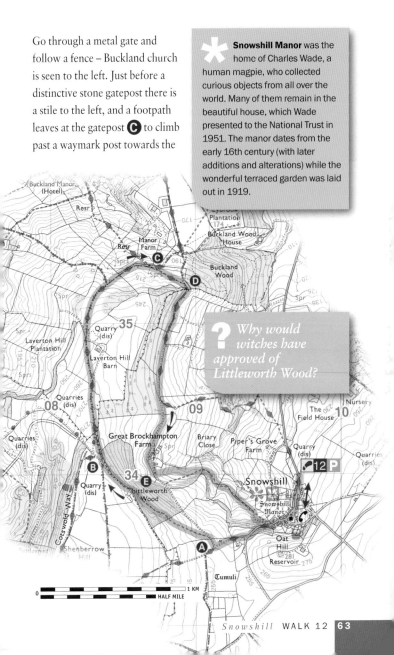

? *Why would witches have approved of Littleworth Wood?*

Snowshill church

lower edge of Buckland Wood.

Cross a stile at the corner of the wood and turn right on to a bridleway **D**. There is an isolated cottage to the left with Snowshill ahead in its picturesque setting. The track is surfaced after the driveway leading to the cottage.

Keep on the lane at Great Brockhampton Farm, and descend to where it merges with a track leading back to farm outbuildings. Go through a gate here **E** to join a well-trodden path that climbs to a gate giving on to an enclosed path.

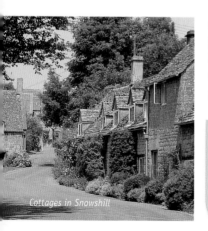
Cottages in Snowshill

A stile leads to a pleasant stretch of grassy walking to pass a pond to the left. The path joins a driveway climbing back to Snowshill. Retrace your steps to the car park. ■

Locals pronounce Snowshill's name as **'Snozzle'**. St Barnabas' Church was completely rebuilt in 1864, only the font surviving from the medieval building.

Batsford from Blockley

- Lovely views
- wonderful trees
- pretty village
- interesting church

Trees must be the theme of this route which takes the walker around the perimeter of one of Britain's most notable arboretums. Batsford's trees have to be admired from afar unless you pay for entry, but footpaths pass by many native trees that have astonishing girth and height. The strenuous sections of the route are separated by sections on a plateau with outstanding views.

walk 13

Near Batsford Park

walk 13

START Blockley Village Shop and Café at centre of village

DISTANCE 4½ miles (7.2km)

TIME 2½ hours

PARKING Street parking in village

ROUTE FEATURES Field paths and tracks with some short, steep sections

GPS WAYPOINTS
- 🖊 SP 164 349
- Ⓐ SP 165 348
- Ⓑ SP 170 346
- Ⓒ SP 191 338
- Ⓓ SP 185 330
- Ⓔ SP 170 341

PUBLIC TRANSPORT Buses from Chipping Campden and Moreton-in-Marsh. Tel. 0871 200 2233

REFRESHMENTS Village Shop and Café, and The Great Western Arms and The Crown Inn at Blockley, tearoom at Batsford Arboretum

PUBLIC TOILETS At start

PLAY AREA None

ORDNANCE SURVEY MAPS Explorer OL45 (The Cotswolds)

🖊 From the Village Shop and Café go into the churchyard. Swing left behind the church, now made famous by the *Father Brown* TV series. Leaving the churchyard, bear right to the main road at the bottom. Turn right and then first left along a street signed to Pasture Farm Ⓐ.

As it degrades to a track, carry on for almost ½ mile (800m). Approaching a large shed Ⓑ,

? *What industry brought prosperity to Blockley during the 18th and 19th centuries?*

branch off ahead beside it and continue climbing at the field edge. Pausing during the ascent, look back for a view to the village. The path is part of the Donnington Way, sponsored by the famous nearby village brewery and waymarked with black spots in white circles.

The view of Blockley from point **E**

> ✱ **Blockley** is a delightfully haphazard village with picturesque cottages spread about the church and neighbouring green.

A glance at the map shows ancient earthworks, and the rough ground where the path follows electric lines to a gate at the top corner of the meadow, may be the hand of man. Carry on beside a row of trees, keeping ahead at a crossing path to continue beside the left hedge. Passing into the next field, watch for the path breaking across right to meet the corner of a lane.

Follow it ahead downhill, passing the Batsford estate offices and former school. Keep going over two crossroads (both roads leading right to

Batsford Park

Batsford's church). About 100 yds past the second crossroads, turn off right through a gate onto a path initially lined with oak.

Batsford Arboretum was created by Lord Redesdale who came to the estate in 1886 having served as a diplomat in Tokyo and China. There are now more than a thousand varieties of trees on display, the colours being particularly spectacular in spring (azaleas, cherries and rhododendron) and autumn. For opening times tel. 01386 701441 or for the café 01386 701974.

Batsford Park is to the right, and walkers may see red deer and the smaller muntjacs as well as birds of prey, whose flying skills are often demonstrated in the park. Keep going beside successive fields for a generous ½ mile (800m) before entering a field by the corner of a small wood D.

Following Monarch's Way signs, turn right along the edge of pasture, corrugated by medieval ridge and furrow ploughing. Towards the far end, skirt a cottage to meet a drive leading to the arboretum. The path continues opposite, moving away from the wall to bypass another cottage.

Walk forward to join a track and maintain the same direction until you reach a fork. Keeping by the estate wall, branch off right, still with the Monarch's Way, to continue climbing beside woodland plantation.

Emerging onto a lane at the top, cross to a narrow track opposite. Leaving the trees, carry on down at the edge of a couple of fields. Meeting a crossing track E, go left, leaving after 100 yds over a stile on the right. With Blockley's church now a landmark, follow a downhill trod to a stile left of Park Farm. Keep going over a crossing track and past a pond to a stile and gate in the far bottom corner. Carry on at the right-hand field edge, finally joining a track out to the road. Go right through the lower village before turning off left to retrace your steps back up to the church.

Lost village of Widford from Burford

- Lost village
- isolated church
- fine manor house
- beautiful riverside

walk 14

Burford is one of the most interesting, historic and beautiful of Cotswold towns. The route begins following the River Windrush to Widford, where there was a sizeable village until the Black Death. After a lovely climb up a hidden valley the walk takes you back via Fulbrook (where it detours to pass the manor house at Westhall Hill).

Burford in spring

START Burford car park

DISTANCE 4½ miles (7.2km)

TIME 2 hours

PARKING At start

ROUTE FEATURES Riverside walking with a few gradients and a succession of stiles; riverside may be wet

GPS WAYPOINTS

🖉 SP 254 122

Ⓐ SP 259 115

Ⓑ SP 271 118

Ⓒ SP 274 120

Ⓓ SP 256 128

Ⓔ SP 250 128

PUBLIC TRANSPORT
Tel. 0871 200 2233

REFRESHMENTS Pub and cafés at Burford, pub at Fulbrook

PUBLIC TOILETS Burford

PLAY AREA None

ORDNANCE SURVEY MAPS
Explorer OL45 (The Cotswolds)

👣 From the car park cross the bridge and turn left to the main road. Go left again opposite the magnificent Great House – like many Burford houses, its classical façade is misleading and screens a house of an earlier time.

Leave the town by a pleasant road lined with picturesque cottages. Soon the houses end and you can look left to where a loop of the River Windrush rejoins the main river.

After some 200 yds along the verge, turn off left over a stile Ⓐ to join a footpath through meadows close to the riverbank. There is a succession of stiles and the surroundings and wildlife provide constant interest. All too soon, the path climbs back to the road.

Follow the road left for a short way and then turn off left to cross the river at Widford Mill.

❓ What connects Native Americans with Henry VIII's barber?

After 200 yds, leave through a gate beside a cattle grid on the right Ⓑ and follow a track to another gate near the 13th-century church of St Oswald. It stands alone above the river, the only building of the medieval village of

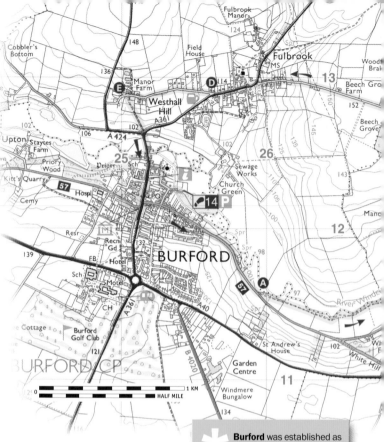

Widford to survive. The village was built on the site of a Roman villa (a fragment of mosaic survives in the chancel of St Oswald's) and was probably abandoned at the time of the Black Death. Leave the track just beyond the gate and walk forward to a waypost **C** near the isolated Shepherd's Cottage. Turn left to another gate and continue up Dean Bottom, a lovely dry valley with woods on both sides above the rich grass.

This part of the walk seems too short before the stile at the top is reached. Turn left on to Blacksmith's Lane – there are good views after Beech Grove Farm, where the descent into Fulbrook begins.

Reaching the main road, turn left to pass the war memorial and continue to a fork **D**. The Carpenters' Arms lies a little farther along the main road, but the route branches off right before it along the lane to Westhall Hill. Walk up to the little hamlet at the end, where there is a remarkable cluster of beautiful old buildings beside the 16th-

Westhall – the manor house

century manor house (not open to the public) with a distinctive archway. The duck pond completes a perfect scene.

You will have to walk back a little way to find a footpath on the right **E** that leaves beside a garage with green doors. The way leads down, stepped at the finish past a wartime pillbox hidden in the trees, to the main road opposite a roundabout.

> **✱** Only lower parts of the tower and west end survive of the church that served Burford in Norman times. After this, bits were added at various levels and in a variety of styles. Nevertheless, **St John the Baptist's Church** is a treasure house to students of church architecture who love the problems it presents. There is a splendid south porch and a wonderful display of monuments. Look for graffiti on the font scratched by a Roundhead kept prisoner in 1649.

Cross, continue over the bridge and then take the first left up Lawrence Lane to the church. Follow a footpath round the churchyard to a small square and walk on past almshouses founded in 1457. Joining Church Lane, go left and wind back to the car park. ■

Church at Widford

Farmington from Northleach

- Beautiful church
- quiet lake
- pretty cross-county trail
- rolling farmland

Northleach was one of the Cotswold's wealthiest towns in the 15th century, and the magnificent church is the testament to this prosperity. The walk takes in the attractive countryside to the east of the town where rolling fields and lush streamside pastures surround the tiny village of Farmington.

walk 15

Northleach

walk 15

START Northleach market square

DISTANCE 5 miles (8km). Shorter version 4 miles (7.2km)

TIME 3 hours (2 hours for shorter route)

PARKING At start

ROUTE FEATURES May be short sections across cultivated land; lack of waymarks

GPS WAYPOINTS
- 📍 SP 113 146
- Ⓐ SP 111 144
- Ⓑ SP 126 138
- Ⓒ SP 134 139
- Ⓓ SP 133 149
- Ⓔ SP 139 147
- Ⓕ SP 135 152
- Ⓖ SP 133 151
- Ⓗ SP 116 147

PUBLIC TRANSPORT Buses from Cheltenham, Cirencester, Moreton-in-Marsh, Oxford and Stow-on-the-Wold. Tel. 0871 200 2233

REFRESHMENTS Sherborne Arms and cafés in Northleach

PUBLIC TOILETS In the market square

PLAY AREA None

ORDNANCE SURVEY MAPS Explorer OL45 (The Cotswolds)

👣 From the market square, walk through the churchyard and turn left almost opposite the porch. Once outside the churchyard turn left and then go right into Mill View. Turn left before the school Ⓐ on to a footpath that crosses a playing field making for the children's playground.

Go through the kissing-gate at the end of the tennis courts to walk through meadows to a lane, reached from the top corner of the last meadow. Turn right and climb uphill.

Just after reaching the crest, turn left into a cul-de-sac. Keep ahead through the gate at the postbox when the lane bends right at

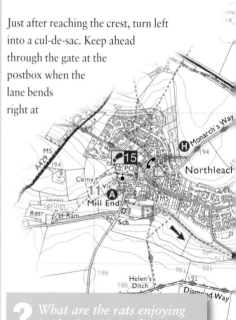

❓ *What are the rats enjoying in the Saints' porch?*

Upper End **B**. Bear right to go down to the bottom end of the lake and cross the bridge over the outfall stream.

Climb the steep track on the other side and go through the metal gate at the top to a farm track. When this goes to the right, walk ahead along a path along a field edge.

Stone from the quarries at **Farmington** was sent to London by road and river to rebuild the city after the Great Fire of 1666. The parish was one of the first in Gloucestershire to be enclosed (in 1713) and the walls put up at this time with stone from the same quarries remain in place today.

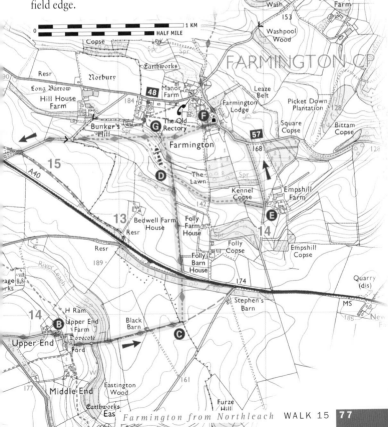

Cottages at Northleach

After a metal gate at the end of the field **C** turn left and cross land to a stile leading into a belt of conifers. Cross the main road and continue on another field-edge path that heads towards Farmington.

The path descends to cross a stream by an iron gate. A few steps farther on there is a footpath junction **D**.

*For the short route keep ahead alongside the fence and then by the edge of the field (there is a drop to the left) to a stile **G** on the left bearing a Monarch's Way emblem.*

To continue on the main route, go through the gate on the right on to The Lawn, a beautiful expanse of pasture descending to a brook. The right of way follows the left bank of the stream until the final field, where it crosses the stream and then reaches a wooden gate giving on to a lane.

Turn left **E** and then, after ½ mile (800m) of easy climbing, left again to Farmington's unpretentious little church. Take the track along the south side of the churchyard following the Monarch's Way. Keep ahead when the track divides. The footpath also divides here **F**.

> ✳ **Northleach** had a brief period of prosperity in the 15th and 16th centuries, when its Church of Saints Peter and Paul was enlarged and beautified, the only hints of the earlier Norman building being the ridge-line of a previous roof on the east side of the tower. The brasses to the memory of Northleach's medieval merchants are outstanding.

St Peter's Church, Farmington

Fork left and head across the large field, keeping to the left of the electric lines. By the time you reach the far side you should be about 100 yds distant from them and will see a shed ahead. Cross the stile here **G**, descend to the bottom of the valley and cross the stream by a footbridge (there is another crossing point farther upstream). From the second bridge climb up the field to its top edge, following the power lines again. Here there is a track that reaches the road by a group of young conifers.

The quiet lane passes beneath the A40. Leave it to the right on to a footpath **H**.

The path descends through trees and then is enclosed through housing. Keep ahead down MacArthur Road, turning left at the bottom into Doctor's Lane, a broad alleyway that leads to Northleach market place. ◼

Woodchester Park

- Five lakes
- striking boathouse
- Woodchester Mansion
- beautiful woodland paths

Situated barely 3 miles (4.8km) to the south of Stroud, Woodchester Park is one of the Cotswolds' secret places. The mansion, in High Gothic style where everything is made of stone, has never been lived in yet stands more or less intact after more than 130 years. The surrounding park has five lakes that look like Scottish lochs, the steep sides of their valley clothed with pines.

The Boathouse

START National Trust car park off Nympsfield – Stroud road

DISTANCE 5 miles (8km)

TIME 3 hours

PARKING At start

ROUTE FEATURES Paths through the National Trust estate are well maintained; a few gradients may be taxing; picnic tables

GPS WAYPOINTS

- SO 798 014
- **Ⓐ** SO 807 013
- **Ⓑ** SO 822 012
- **Ⓒ** SO 825 012
- **Ⓓ** SO 822 011
- **Ⓔ** SO 817 013
- **Ⓕ** SO 812 014

PUBLIC TRANSPORT None

REFRESHMENTS None en route; Rose and Crown at Nympsfield

PUBLIC TOILETS At Mansion when open to public

PLAY AREA None

ORDNANCE SURVEY MAPS Explorer 168 (Stroud, Tetbury & Malmesbury), Landranger 163 (Cheltenham & Cirencester)

 The steps that descend from the car park take you to a woodland track that steadily drops down to a delightful pastoral valley. Follow pink waymarks and fork left at a gate when the track divides at the bottom **Ⓐ**.

The track goes behind the Mansion, passing remains of outbuildings on the left and the remains of the former terraced gardens to the right. The climb continues through woodland before descending to a junction where you get a glimpse of the main house on the right.

Woodchester Mansion is a romantic building. In 1845 William Leigh bought the estate (embracing five parishes) for £100,000. He had recently become a Roman Catholic and commissioned designs for two projects – a country house for himself and a church and monastery on a different site.

Pugin and Charles Francis Hansom produced drawings for **Woodchester Mansion** but their work was rejected in favour of a 21-year-old local architect, Benjamin Bucknall. He was a disciple of Viollet-le-Duc, an expert on Gothic architecture. On Leigh's death in 1873, after 16 years' work, the project was abandoned overnight, leaving scaffolding erected and tools where they lay. Fortunately, the roof had been completed. Visitors may tour the house at weekends in summer. For opening times tel. 01453 861541.

A gargoyle at Woodchester Mansion, inspired by those made by Viollet-le-Duc for Notre Dame Cathedral, Paris

Turn left here, looking out for waymarks. Continue to follow them on the main track when the red route leaves to the left above Honeywell Pond. After 200 yds bear right as the track descends, steeply at first and then more gently. As it bends right, branch left at an orange waymark. Keep ahead **B**, now following the red waymark.

The red route goes to the left **C** at a T-junction. Leave it by turning right on a track that soon gives views of Kennel Pond, separated from Parkmill Pond by a narrow causeway.

Turn right to cross the end of Parkmill Pond to follow pink waymarks again. A waterfall can be seen some distance up the lake

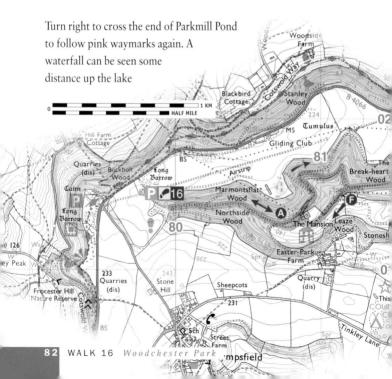

from the dam. Turn right again to walk up the track on the south side of Parkmill Pond. This side of the lake is much more enclosed by trees.

Bear right to pass The Old Kennels, an open shed with picnic tables, but do not cross the causeway. Turn left **D** to continue along the south side of Middle Pond, joining a good path crossing an open grassy area, a former poplar plantation. On the far side of this a kissing-gate opens on to a more narrow path with wooden steps and plankwalks over difficult ground.

The picturesque Boathouse stands by the causeway separating Old Pond from Middle Pond **E**. Cross the causeway and turn left along a shoreline path that leads up steps to a driveway followed earlier. Keep left here. After about 300 yds keep ahead to follow pink/red waymarks to go through a gate **F** on to a track that will take you past the Mansion and on to the main track that climbs steadily to the car park. ■

> **?** What will you not find at Woodchester Mansion because Viollet-le-Duc deplored it?

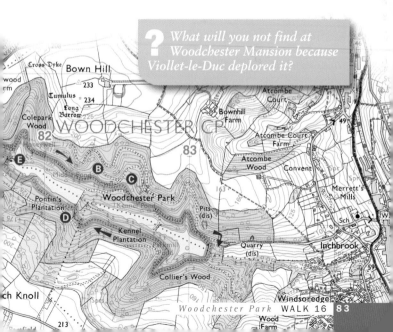

The Slaughters from Bourton-on-the-Water

- ▥ Mill and museum
- ▥ riverside walking
- ▥ two long-distance trails
- ▥ three famous villages

walk 17

Upper and Lower Slaughter have featured on countless calendars through the years, the pictures usually showing honey-coloured cottages and the quaint foot-bridges that span the tiny River Eye. The walk offers many different vistas of the villages, while Bourton-on-the Water, hardly less famous, also reveals an unexpected beauty spot.

Lower Slaughter

START Bourton-on-the-Water church

DISTANCE 5 miles (8km). Shorter version 4 miles (6.4km)

TIME $2\frac{1}{2}$ hours (2 hours for shorter route)

PARKING Public car parks in Bourton

ROUTE FEATURES Stretches may be muddy; steady climb out of valley

GPS WAYPOINTS

- SP 166 208
- Ⓐ SP 166 206
- Ⓑ SP 151 212
- Ⓒ SP 153 218
- Ⓓ SP 160 222
- Ⓔ SP 154 231
- Ⓕ SP 157 232
- Ⓖ SP 165 222
- Ⓗ SP 168 212

PUBLIC TRANSPORT Buses from Cirencester, Moreton-in-Marsh, Stow-on-the-Wold, Cheltenham and Northleach. Tel. 0871 200 2233

REFRESHMENTS Old Mill tearoom at Lower Slaughter; pubs and cafés in Bourton-on-the-Water

PUBLIC TOILETS At village centre next to Edinburgh Woollen Mills shop

PLAY AREA None

ORDNANCE SURVEY MAPS Explorer OL45 (The Cotswolds)

From the church turn left along Bourton's main street and then cross the River Windrush by the bridge opposite the Old Manse Hotel. Pass the Bakery on the Water and turn right on to a narrow footpath Ⓐ (the start of the Windrush Way) where the road divides at The Warren. The twisting path suddenly emerges into a lovely riverside meadow – a delightful surprise that must be Bourton's best-kept secret. All too soon the path by the river reaches the road. Turn left to come to the A429 (Fosse Way).

Cross the main road by the bridge that bears a plaque showing the badge of the Second Legion, who were responsible for building the Fosse Way. Take the footpath on the east side of the Windrush, which at first follows it closely through a meadow. At the end of the meadow the path follows a field-edge track and rises to skirt a wood. If it has been wet and used by horses this short stretch of the route may be muddy. It is hard to see exactly where the path crossed the former Cheltenham to

? *What group of people built the Fosse Way?*

Chipping Norton railway line, but soon after this the path divides. Turn right on to the Gloucestershire Way **B**, turning your back to the River Windrush and beginning to climb the side of the valley.

After about ½ mile (800m) look for a metal gate on the right **C** that marks the start of another bridleway heading across a field

✳ The best way of seeing **Upper Slaughter** is on foot as car parking is practically non-existent. The footpaths on the return leg of the walk go through 'the slough' that gives the village its name, though the boggy area has been made into comparatively well-drained water meadows. The village is built around the site of a Norman castle, and the church dates from the same era, though this is disguised by 19th-century restoration.

(part of the Macmillan Way). Cross a road and continue on the bridleway, looking down to Bourton on the right and then to Lower Slaughter ahead. The bridleway comes to a crossways **D**.

*If you wish to take the shorter route, not visiting Upper Slaughter, keep ahead to the centre of Lower Slaughter. Turn right to follow the river and reach **G**.*

To continue on the main route, turn left along the lane, admiring an ever-changing vista of Lower Slaughter, the church distinctive with the

Bourton-on-the-Water

top of its spire dressed with new stone. Keep ahead when you reach a T-junction. Now you can see Upper Slaughter and the Lords of the Manor Hotel that dates from the 17th century and once served as the rectory. Pass the road to Guiting Power and turn right **E** into Upper Slaughter village, passing

the church in a beautiful position set back from the cottages surrounding a small square. Bear left to pass the former village school where the famous view of the River Eye and the little bridges is revealed.

Cross the river: you may like to take the riverside footpath if dry conditions prevail *(but avoid it if it is at all wet – the path is becoming eroded)*. Otherwise follow the road that runs parallel, turn left before the bridge and climb 100 yds up the road. Where it swings left, go through an iron gate **F** into a meadow and bear right to find another iron gate that takes the path on through a long meadow. There is a fine view of the hotel across a pond.

A kissing-gate at the end of the meadow gives on to a riverside path leading into Lower Slaughter. Turn right at the road to reach the mill (that houses a museum) and then turn left to walk by the river through the village. Bear right almost opposite the church to continue on the left-hand bank of the river for about 100 yds by the road. Take the footpath on the right to leave the road and then keep ahead (now leaving the river) when a footpath goes off to the left.

After a metal gate **G**, bear left on the surfaced footpath that follows a hedge at first and then crosses fields to reach the main road almost opposite the Coach and Horses. Turn right, and then, after 100 yds, left into Bourton.

Pass Meadow Way on the left and, where the road bends right, take the footpath on the right **H** past a bungalow named Altamara. The footpath goes between a school and its playing field and soon reaches the church. ■

Winchcombe and Hailes Abbey

- ▨ Historic wool town
- ▨ Puck Pit Lane
- ▨ medieval abbey ruins
- ▨ delightful countryside

This is a walk of several options. The way to Hailes Abbey is along Puck Pit Lane (as charming as its name suggests) and then by field paths. The leg up Salter's Lane and Fluke's Hill is more demanding with steady climbs and muddy descents. The beautiful pastures and woodland that the path goes through, and far-reaching views, makes the effort worthwhile.

walk 18

Cottages at Winchcombe

walk 18

START Winchcombe – top of Castle Street

DISTANCE 5 miles (8km)

TIME 3 hours

PARKING On-street parking in Winchcombe or car park near library

ROUTE FEATURES Comparatively easy going outward but the return is more demanding with steady climbs and muddy descents

GPS WAYPOINTS
- 🖉 SP 024 282
- Ⓐ SP 027 282
- Ⓑ SP 028 288
- Ⓒ SP 038 294
- Ⓓ SP 047 300
- Ⓔ SP 048 288
- Ⓕ SP 034 287

PUBLIC TRANSPORT Tel. 0871 200 2233

REFRESHMENTS Pubs and tearooms in Winchcombe

PUBLIC TOILETS At Winchcombe and Hailes Abbey

PLAY AREA None

ORDNANCE SURVEY MAPS Explorer OL45 (The Cotswolds)

👣 Turn down Castle Street by the White Hart and cross the concealed bridge that takes the road over the little River Isbourne. Turn left up an alleyway Ⓐ, following the Gloucestershire Way sign.

A kissing-gate takes the path into a riverside meadow with the medieval pattern of ridge-and-furrow cultivation clearly visible. Cross a footbridge and walk through two more meadows to a road. Bear right to follow the main road for 100 yds before turning right by the 30 mph sign into Puck Pit Lane Ⓑ.

This lovely byway is part of the Cotswold Way and gives views over fields and woodland. Once English main roads were like this. When the lane ends, continue over a stile.

Cross a meadow heading to the left of a rusty-roofed cowshed and go through a kissing-gate **C** into another meadow. There are views of lovely countryside to the left as you cross the next field to a kissing-gate near the lower corner, where the ground quickly becomes muddy after wet weather.

Walk through the long meadow – a footpath crosses from the left – to reach a gate at the far end. From here the right of way goes across a

> **Salt** has been a vital commodity in England throughout history to preserve food through winter and spring. Most salt originated from Droitwich, and the Salt Way passed through the Cotswolds from Worcester to reach the Thames at Lechlade.

> **?** *Who was Puck?*

Above Winchcombe

field to a field-edge track that leads to a wide farm track. Turn left on to this and turn right at the lane. After 150 yds the Cotswold Way leaves to the left **D** – follow it for ¼ mile (400m) to Hailes Abbey.

After your visit to the abbey, return to the lane and turn left (here named Salter's Lane; it is a continuation of the ancient Salt Way). The climb is easy at first but the way becomes steadily steeper as the lane passes Haile on the Hill and approaches woods. After about 20 minutes of exertion, turn right through an iron gate near the top just before trees **E**.

The route again becomes part of the Gloucestershire Way – a lovely path along the flank of Fluke's Hill. Go through a galvanised

> **Hailes Abbey** (National Trust) was founded in 1246 by Richard, Earl of Cornwall, as thanks after having been saved from shipwreck. Cistercian monks were brought from Beaulieu to run the abbey, which quickly became wealthy and powerful. This was helped by its famous relic, a phial of Holy Blood that attracted pilgrims from near and far. Chaucer's Pardoner mentions it in his *Canterbury Tale*. Only parts of the cloisters survive, though the other abbey buildings are marked on the ground, and there is a fascinating museum.

gate, then turn left when the path divides at a wooden gate and climb a steep slope to a stile into a wood. Steps lead down an equally steep bank. There follows a lovely section of grassy walking, descending gently and looking for a gate to the right with Winchcombe visible beyond.

From the gate the path descends another steep slope where there are flights of steps to help *(but the going may still be slippery)*. Better grassy walking follows with views of Winchcombe from near the first of a series of metal kissing-gates.

*No stones are standing now of the great Benedictine **abbey** that dominated **Winchcombe**. It was founded by Kenulph, King of Mercia, in 811. After his son Kenelm was murdered by his wicked sister (who had her eyes torn out in an act of divine intervention) the abbey attracted crowds of pilgrims who believed that Kenelm's shrine had powerful holy properties. In 1539 the abbey was dissolved and the land and buildings given to the Seymours of Sudeley Castle. St Peter's Church was built about 1460 when the abbey was in its heyday. It has a fine tower, broad nave and beautiful organ case.*

Cross a lane **F** into a pasture. The right of way (diverted to pass to the left of Stancombe Farm) is well marked by large plates of white plastic. When the diversion ends, head for Winchcombe across a large field.

Turn left at a lane and after 50 yds go through a wooden gate on the right to cross the water meadow diagonally to the end of the alleyway used at the beginning of the route. At the road, turn right to return to the centre of the village of Winchcombe. ■

Hailes Abbey

Guiting Wood

- Picturesque valley
- woodland walk
- site of medieval village
- verdant countryside

An advantage of this route is that you may like to undertake it in two parts – there is a small, isolated car park just off Critchford Lane where you can leave the car close to the halfway point. The walk will be particularly rewarding in spring or autumn when foliage is at its most colourful. If you have to ask for directions note that Guiting is pronounced 'guyting'.

War memorial at Guiting Power

walk 19

START Guiting Power

DISTANCE 6¼ miles (10.1km)

TIME 3½ hours

PARKING Village hall car park, Guiting Power (near church)

ROUTE FEATURES Some steeper and potential muddy paths in the woodland section

GPS WAYPOINTS
SP 094 246
Ⓐ SP 095 250
Ⓑ SP 084 258
Ⓒ SP 079 270
Ⓓ SP 070 269
Ⓔ SP 066 264
Ⓕ SP 072 260
Ⓖ SP 089 252

PUBLIC TRANSPORT Tel. 0871 200 2233

REFRESHMENTS The Farmers Arms and The Hollow Bottom at Guiting Power

PUBLIC TOILETS None

PLAY AREA None

ORDNANCE SURVEY MAPS Explorer OL45 (The Cotswolds)

From the car park walk back to the village centre by the war memorial. Take the cul-de-sac diagonally opposite, following it to a kissing-gate at the end. The ongoing path accompanies a stream to a footbridge spanning a tributary of the River Windrush, climbing beyond to a fork Ⓐ.

Bear right through a gate into a meadow and walk away by the left hedge. Keep ahead beyond its corner to a kissing-gate at the far side, from where the view back is along the beautiful Windrush Valley. Walk ahead at the edge of small paddocks to Little Windrush Farm. Follow the ongoing track to a junction and go left. There are good views of Guiting Wood (and the Manor House) as you pass Castlett Farm (note its fine barn). The fields beyond to the left were the site of a medieval hamlet, although its outlines have been lost to the plough.

At the end, turn left along Critchford Lane. After a ford and small footbridge, the lane rises to a junction by a barn and the small car park previously mentioned as an alternative start Ⓑ.

? *What is a fulling mill?*

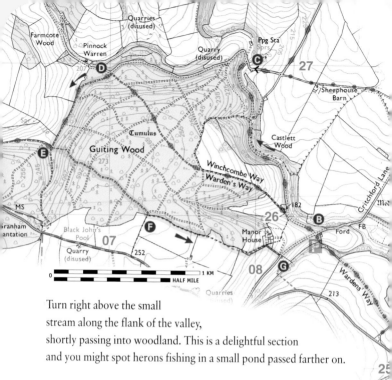

Turn right above the small
stream along the flank of the valley,
shortly passing into woodland. This is a delightful section
and you might spot herons fishing in a small pond passed farther on.

Reaching a T-junction **C**, go left to begin a steep climb. However, it
soon eases and the lane meanders along the pleasant valley for ¾ mile
(1.2km) to a sharp right-hand bend **D**. Leave through a gate onto the
Farmcote Estate and follow a broad, gravel track right, signed the
Wardens Way, along the bottom edge of Guiting Wood. Shortly after a
drive off right to Farmcote Wood Farm, watch for a crossing footpath **E**.

Take the narrow path off to the left, which climbs steeply into the trees.
Higher up, after the gradient eases, keep ahead across a grass horse ride,
and farther on, over an estate track. In a little while the way leads to a
kissing-gate, emerging from the wood onto the edge of a field **F**.

Go left, gently descending along the boundaries of successive fields,
from where there is a grand view across the rolling Cotswold

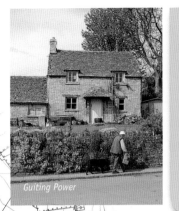
Guiting Power

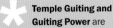
Temple Guiting and Guiting Power are neighbouring villages in the Windrush Valley. It is easy to see how Temple Guiting came by its name – the land here belonged to the Knights Templar. Less easily explained is Guiting Power. Although it could have referred to the fulling mills that were a feature of the valley from Norman times onwards, in fact it takes the name of a local family. 'Guiting' is from an Old English word meaning a flood.

countryside. Lower down, the slope steepens and the path angles round towards the Manor House, which has an unusual lantern on the roof. Meeting its drive, turn down to Critchford Lane and go left, back to the junction passed earlier **B**.

Turn right just before the car park to follow the Wardens' Way on a descending track. Climb away between the fields to its end at a T-junction opposite barns **G**.

Turn left on a rough track dropping into trees, which curves past a ford to continue as a narrower path, rising above the stream along the valley. Eventually breaking from the trees, carry on and join a lane that leads back to the main street in Guiting Power. Go left to the war memorial and then right to return to the village hall and the starting point. ∎

Bibury and Coln St Aldwyns

- Picture-book village
- 14th-century cottages
- beautiful riverside
- meadows and woodland

walk 20

Bibury is one of the 'must see' Cotswold places. The riverside walk to Coln St Aldwyns, another delightful village, is through verdant countryside at its best in summer. The return is mainly on a bridleway across pastureland. The place names may be confusing – Bibury is on the north bank of the River Coln, Arlington on the south, Ablington is just a mile (1.6km) upstream.

The River Coln and Bibury Court

walk 20

START Arlington Mill

DISTANCE 6³/₄ miles (10.9km)

TIME 3½ hours

PARKING Finding space at Bibury can be difficult at peak times. There is a small car park opposite Arlington Mill, roadside parking by the river and byway parking in streets near the church

ROUTE FEATURES Some gradients and footpaths across cultivated land

GPS WAYPOINTS
🔲 SP 114 068
Ⓐ SP 111 066
Ⓑ SP 124 055
Ⓒ SP 143 047
Ⓓ SP 127 048

PUBLIC TRANSPORT Tel. 0871 200 2233

REFRESHMENTS Pubs at Bibury and Coln St Aldwyns

PUBLIC TOILETS On Bibury main street

PLAY AREA None

ORDNANCE SURVEY MAPS Explorer OL45 (The Cotswolds)

🔲 With Arlington Mill to the right, climb along the main road away from the River Coln past The Catherine Wheel inn. Take the footpath on the left immediately after Ⓐ and climb by the left boundary to a gate and stone stile.

Over the stile, follow a track right to the next bend. Leave there through a gap ahead into a field corner and turn left to walk away with a hedge on your left. In the corner, keep ahead as the path becomes enclosed, later running beside a wood and reaching a junction.

Bear right and follow the ongoing path above the steep bank of Oxhill Wood, in time passing through a gate and descending to a stone stile and footbridge Ⓑ. Bear left across open meadow, skirting the foot of a grass bank to a gate at the corner of Ash Copse. A track continues beside the wood, emerging into more meadow beyond. Through a gate, carry on at the edge of two cultivated fields to a fork. There branch right from the river, an open field now on your left and a wood shortly materialising on your right. After then passing through the wood, carry on across another pleasant meadow. Closing with the river at its far end, bear left at a signpost and walk out through gates past Yew Tree Lodge onto a lane Ⓒ.

Turn left, cross the river and immediately go left again onto a driveway. Just before gates to Mill House, leave right across a footbridge. A path climbs away to the end of a lane. Follow it past the former vicarage to a junction, where St John's Church lies to the left. The onward route, however, is ahead, past a row of almshouses built with stone and timber from the demolished Victorian wings of Williamstrip House in 1947.

Keep right at the next junction to a crossroads by the Post Office. Turn right towards Quenington, passing the New Inn on the left. Leaving the village, the lane swings right, taking you back to the bridge across the River Coln **C**.

Return past the lodge into the park, but this time walk forward at the signpost. Follow a gently climbing trod between ash and beech, later accompanying a wall.

Through a gate at the end, carry on across cultivated fields to a track at the far side. Walk ahead past a cottage and continue across a small paddock beyond to a gate. Keep going along the length of large meadow to emerge at the far left corner onto a lane. Turn right past a lodge and then immediately go right again onto a track **D**.

In spring, bluebells fringe the track, which crosses the line of Akeman Street, a Roman road that ran from St Albans to Cirencester. Their road may have followed an even more ancient track and although it remained in use throughout the subsequent Saxon era, there is now no obvious trace of this section on the ground. Reaching a fork, branch left into Ash Copse and head down through the trees. Emerging into a meadow at the bottom, continue downhill to reach the footbridge crossed earlier **B**. Climb away beyond, and retrace your steps above Oxhill Wood. Reaching a fork, now go right, passing through a gate and heading down between fields towards Court Farm and the river. Wind past the old mill and across the Coln, beyond which is a fine view to

? *Which well-known cleric is connected with Coln St Aldwyns?*

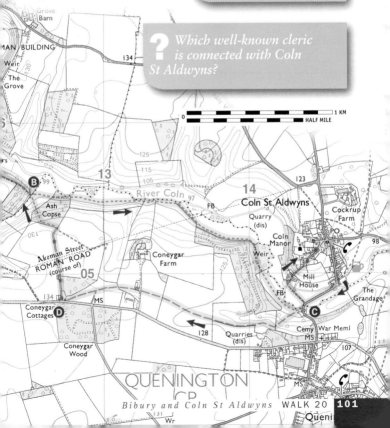

Bibury Court as the drive leads out to a lane.

Turn left at the lane and left again with the main road. However, leave just around the bend, branching off left, not along the street, but through a gap and past a red telephone box beside the right edge of a small green, The Square. Continue down past cottages to a little square by the church. Bear right along Church Road to return to the main road.

Bibury was acclaimed by William Morris as the most beautiful village in England and thousands of tourists spend moments here each year before dashing off to new beauty spots. The walker who lingers here will discover a lovely church with Saxon details, a famous inn, picturesque mills, and quiet corners like The Square occupied by delightful cottages. There is also Bibury Court, a Tudor building enlarged by Sir Thomas Sackville in 1633 and now a hotel.

Follow it ahead to the Post Office, just beyond which is an old footbridge across the river to Arlington Row, Bibury's world-famous terrace of 14th-century cottages. At the end of the row, go right on a surfaced path that borders an old water meadow known as Rack Isle, where cloth dyed at Arlington Mill was once dried. The footpath returns you to the roadside car park opposite Arlington Mill. ■

Arlington Row

Further Information

Walking Safety

Although the reasonably gentle countryside that is the subject of this book offers no real dangers to walkers at any time of the year, it is still advisable to take sensible precautions and follow certain well-tried guidelines.

Always take with you both warm and waterproof clothing and sufficient food and drink. Wear suitable footwear such as strong walking boots or shoes that give a good grip over stony ground, on

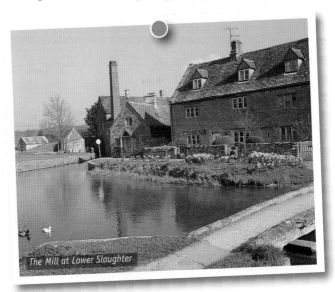
The Mill at Lower Slaughter

slippery slopes and in muddy conditions. Try to obtain a local weather forecast and bear it in mind before you start. Do not be afraid to abandon your proposed route and return to your starting point in the event of a sudden and unexpected deterioration in the weather.

All the walks described in this book will be safe to do, given due care and respect, even during the winter. Indeed, a crisp, fine winter day often provides perfect walking conditions, with firm ground underfoot and a clarity unique to this time of the year.

The most difficult hazard likely to be encountered is mud, especially when walking along woodland and field paths, farm tracks and bridleways – the latter in particular can often get churned up by cyclists and horses. In summer, an additional difficulty may be narrow and overgrown paths, particularly along the edges of cultivated fields. Neither should constitute a major problem provided that the appropriate footwear is worn.

Bluebells in Sherborne Park

Global Positioning System (GPS)

What is GPS?

Global Positioning System, or GPS for short, is a fully-functional navigation system that uses a network of satellites to calculate positions, which are then transmitted to hand-held receivers. By measuring the time it takes a signal to reach the receiver, the distance from the satellite can be estimated. Repeat this with several satellites and the receiver can then triangulate its position, in effect telling the receiver exactly where you are, in any weather, day or night, anywhere on Earth.

GPS co-ordinates, in the form of waypoint grid references, are used in Pathfinder® guidebooks, and many readers find the positional accuracy GPS affords a reassurance, although its greatest benefit comes when you are walking in remote, open countryside or through forests.

GPS has become a vital global utility, indispensable for modern navigation on land, sea and air around the world, as well as an important tool for map-making and land surveying.

Period houses in Park Street, Cirencester

Follow the Country Code

- Be safe – plan ahead and follow any signs
- Leave gates and property as you find them
- Protect plants and animals, and take your litter home
- Keep dogs under close control
- Consider other people

(Natural England)

Useful Organisations

Campaign to Protect Rural England
5-11 Lavington Street,
London, SE1 0NZ
Tel. 020 7981 2800
www.cpre.org.uk

Cotswold District Council
www.cotswold.gov.uk/go/tourism

English Heritage
The Engine House,
Fire Fly Avenue,
Swindon SN2 2EH
Tel. 01793 414700
www.english-heritage.org.uk

Forestry Commission England
South West of England regional office
Buller's Hill, Kennford,
Exeter,
EX6 7XR
Tel. 0300 067 4960
www.forestry.gov.uk

Gloucestershire County Council
Environment Department
Tel. 01452 425000
www.gloucestershire.gov.uk/environment

National Trust
Membership and general enquiries:
Tel. 0344 800 1895
www.nationaltrust.org.uk
Regional Office
Gloucestershire and Somerset:
Unit 3, The Hubbard Wing,
Leigh Court, Pill road,
Abbots Leigh, BS8 3RJ,
Tel. 01275 378440

Natural England
Tel. 0300 060 3900
www.gov.uk/government/organisat
ions/natural-england

Ordnance Survey
Tel. 03456 05 05 05
www.ordnancesurvey.co.uk

Oxfordshire County Council
Countryside Service
Tel. 01865 810226
www.oxfordshire.gov.uk/countyside

Ramblers
2nd Floor, Camelford House,
87–90 Albert Embankment,
London SE1 7TW
Tel. 020 7339 8500
www.ramblers.org.uk

Tourist Information
www.cotswolds.com
www.visitcotswolds.co.uk
Local tourist information centres
Abingdon: 01235 522711
Bourton-on-the-Water:
01451 820211
Burford: 01993 823558
Cheltenham: 01242 387492
Chipping Campden:
01386 841206
Cirencester: 01285 654180
Gloucester: 01452 396572
Lechlade: 01367 252631

Moreton in Marsh: 01608 650881
Nailsworth: 01453 839222
Stow-on-the-Wold: 01451 870998
Stroud: 01453 760960
Tetbury: 01666 503552
Tewkesbury: 01684 855040
Winchcombe: 01242 602925

Traveline: 0871 200 2233

Youth Hostels Association
Trevelyan House, Dimple Road,
Matlock, Derbyshire DE4 3YH
Tel. 01629 592700
www.yha.org.uk

*Ordnance Survey maps
of the Cotswolds*
Explorer maps:
OL45 (The Cotswolds)
168 (Stroud, Tetbury & Malmesbury)
179 (Gloucester, Cheltenham &
Stroud)
Landranger maps:
163 (Cheltenham & Cirencester)

Answers to Questions

Walk 1: Workmen would collect ice from lakes and ponds during the winter and it would be stored underground in the ice-house.

Walk 2: The 132ft- (40m) high tower, built in 1400, was funded by the properties of the earls of Kent and Salisbury, who rebelled against Henry IV but were captured and beheaded by citizens.

Walk 3: On the estate cottages opposite The Victoria inn.

High ground on the return leg of the Cleeve Hill walk

Walk 4: The distinctive scratches show that badgers often clamber over this stone stile.

Walk 5: To a water deity.

Walk 6: Many famous jockeys used to train on Cleeve Common, among them Fred Archer, whose ghost is supposed to haunt Prestbury.

Walk 7: Thirteen people.

Walk 8: The fearsome gargoyles on St Lawrence's Church.

Walk 9: Edward Thomas made Adlestrop famous by describing an unscheduled halt when he was on his way to visit his friend and fellow poet Robert Frost.

> *Yes I remember Adlestrop –*
> *The name, because one afternoon*
> *Of heat the express train drew up there*
> *Unwontedly. It was late June.*
> *The steam hissed. Someone cleared his throat.*
> *No one left and no one came*
> *On the bare platform. What I saw*
> *Was Adlestrop – only the name.*

Subsequently Thomas was killed in France on April 9, 1917.

Walk 10: Cliff Well carries the inscription:

> *Go seek that well which never faileth.*

Walk 11: Holy Trinity Church reflects the Minchinhampton's importance in the wool trade.

Walk 12: Littleworth Wood is coppiced woodland. The slender growth of ash is now used for fencing or thatching but was previously made into broomsticks.

Walk 13: Several of its mills were converted to silk throwing to provide yarn for Coventry's silk ribbon industry.

Walk 14: A monument in St John the Baptist's Church to Edmund Harman, who was Henry VIII's barber, has Native Americans dancing around the lettering.

Walk 15: There is a delightful carving in the porch of the Church of

Saints Peter and Paul of a cat playing a fiddle to three rats.

Walk 16: Viollet-le-Duc deplored the use of wood or metal in Gothic revival buildings.

Walk 17: The Roman Second Legion – no doubt with many British slaves.

Walk 18: A mischievous or evil spirit, immortalised in Shakespeare's *A Midsummer Night's Dream*.

Walk 19: A mill where woollen cloth was cleaned and thickened.

Walk 20: John Keble (1792-1866), a founder of the Oxford Movement and author of *The Christian Year* was curate for 10 years. Keble College at Oxford was founded in his memory.

Ordnance Survey

Pathfinder® Guides — Britain's best-loved walking guides

South West of England

Pathfinder Walks

Short Walks

South East of England

Pathfinder Walks

Short Walks

Practical Guide

City Walks

For more information visit

www.pathfinderwalks.co.uk
tel: 01225 584 950
email: info@pathfinderwalks.co.uk
Twitter: @PathfinderWalks
Facebook: www.facebook.com/pathfinderwalks